Dump *for* Diabetics

TELEBrands **PRESS**

TELEBrands PRESS

Telebrands Press
79 Two Bridges Road
Fairfield, NJ 07004

ISBN: 978-0-9972597-0-4

Printed in USA

10 9 8 7 6 5 4

About Cathy

Cathy has been cooking for 60 years, starting at her Grandmother's side, standing on a stool. She never refers to herself as a chef, but rather a great home cook who enjoys making simple, easy meals with ordinary ingredients. She has been sharing those ideas on television since her first commercial in 1989, introducing America to the electric sandwich maker, and in typical Cathy fashion, making a lot more than sandwiches.

Her kitchen has always been the gathering place for friends and family and she loves to share her recipes and cooking hints while she prepares meals or snacks, often testing out new recipes on a willing group of "Tasters." She has an extended family of 5 adult children, ranging in age from 34 to 46, and 10 grandkids from 4 to 23. One of her favorite stories is overhearing her oldest son's response, when a dinner guest commented before dinner that he didn't really like something on the menu.

He said, "Well maybe not before, but you haven't tried my Mom's yet!"

Cathy was diagnosed with type 2 diabetes but thanks to her recipes and regular exercise she is now able to manage it without medication.

Contents

Introduction to Diabetes

What is Diabetes?

If you or someone you care about has diabetes, you probably know that it's a problem with insulin production or sensitivity. The pancreas makes insulin that helps your body's cells absorb the glucose (sugar) that comes from your food. Your body's cells need to absorb the glucose in your blood to give you energy. When your body doesn't make enough insulin to absorb the glucose or your body's cells aren't responding to the insulin very well, your blood sugar levels can rise to dangerous levels. Type 2 is by far the most common type of diabetes in the United States, but Type 1 diabetes (more common in children and adolescents) and Gestational diabetes (a form of diabetes that occurs during pregnancy) are also serious health issues.

There are a few ways that doctors recommend treating Type 2 diabetes. Depending on the person, lifestyle changes, medicine, and/or insulin may be recommended.

Treating diabetes early with healthy eating and exercise helps regulate blood glucose levels and keep serious complications from developing.

What Do I Do Now that I Have Diabetes?

If you are struggling with diabetes, it's important to know that you are not alone. Millions of Americans are learning to live with this disease and are making changes to eat healthier. There are so many ways that you can take action to keep this disease from taking over your life. You already know that exercise is a fantastic way to keep you happy and healthy. For those with diabetes, it's even more crucial. It promotes blood flow, draws the extra glucose out of your blood stream, and helps your body's cells provide you with the energy you need.

Can I Still Eat the Foods I Love?

This is a common worry for people who have diabetes. Along with exercise, eating healthy is essential for maintaining your blood sugar level. The good news is: You can still eat the foods you love! My collection of *Dump for Diabetics* is designed with you in mind, because everyone deserves to enjoy exciting foods every day.

Dump for Diabetics takes the stress out of planning meals for healthy living. Here you have over 200 recipes to satisfy your appetite without a lot of fancy ingredients or extra steps. Just dump the ingredients together, cook them to perfection in a skillet, casserole dish, or slow cooker, and sit down to a nutritious update of your favorite comfort foods. Because nutritional information is provided for each recipe, you can easily track your daily intake of carbohydrates, saturated fats, sodium, etc. to ensure that you're sticking to your doctor's guidelines. Soon you'll be an expert in throwing together quick, healthy meals that make you feel good.

What's the Deal with Carbs?

Carbohydrates enter your body and break down into glucose. People with diabetes have too much glucose in their bloodstream and not enough in their cells. Because of this, they need to avoid eating too many carbs at once. To help your body manage the amount of glucose in the bloodstream, it's important that you're aware of when you eat carbs and how many grams of carbs you eat daily. The key thing to remember is that you don't have to remove all carbs from your diet. They are an excellent source of energy and you need them. Your goal is to try to eat the same amount of carbs at around the same time every day.

If you're counting carbohydrates, you probably have a target range of how many carbs you can eat per meal. A general rule of thumb for a woman (who isn't trying to lose weight) is 45-60 grams of carbs per meal. For men, it's 60-75 grams of carbs per meal. Those who are trying to lose weight may have a lower target range. Use the nutritional information provided with each of the recipes in this book to stay within this targeted area.

Can I Still Eat Dessert?

It's tough to imagine a life without dessert, but many of the desserts we know and love (and the ones we order at restaurants) are way too high in carbohydrates and sugar to eat every day. When you have diabetes, desserts can still be part of life but they need to be treated as a special prize. Thankfully, *Dump for Diabetics* features 100 delicious, low-carb desserts and they can all be yours! All you have to do is some simple planning. If you're aiming to stay within 45-60 carbs per meal, then remember to factor in dessert when you're choosing your meal.

Take the Taco Casserole on page 26 for example. It's only 33 grams of carbs! That means you can enjoy it tonight for dinner and still indulge in a scrumptious, pudding-filled, Chocolate Chip Graham Sandwich (page 205) for only 23 additional grams of carbs for a grand total of 56 carbs. That keeps you well satisfied and well within the 60 carb-per-meal limit. There are plenty of tasty dump dinners and desserts to pair together in the pages that follow, plus some bonus side dishes to shake things up. Have fun choosing your favorite combinations every day!

Do I Need Fancy Ingredients to Make These Recipes?

You don't need fancy ingredients to make these recipes. You'll notice that many of them use reduced-sodium, low-fat, and/or sugar-free variations of your favorite pantry products. Walk down any grocery store aisle and you'll realize how easy it is to find these products. Stock up on items like low-sodium broths, low-fat cheese, sugar-free marinades, sugar-free cake mixes (for dessert), and you've got the beginnings of some fantastic recipes.

Sugar substitutes like Splenda and Sweet 'N Low are just the thing when a recipe calls for a teaspoon or two of sugar, but for recipes that call for more sugar, you'll want to stock your pantry with a bag of "sugar blend." This easy-to-find ingredient is a combination of artificial sweetener and real sugar and it comes in very handy for making desserts with just the right flavor.

How Much is Too Much?

Portion control is key when you're a diabetic. I've kept the portion sizes in the *Dump for Diabetics* recipes small but reasonable so that you are satisfied but not stuffed at the end of a meal or dessert. The detailed nutritional information that follows each recipe will include the Total Carbohydrates per serving, so it's easy to count carbs, track what you eat and keep your blood sugar level under control. Get ready to feel good about your meal choices and eat the foods you love with less guilt.

I'm Too Busy to Track My Eating

Counting carbs and keeping a food log may seem like an overwhelming task at first, but it's easy to fit it into your day once you get in the habit. To help you get started, *Dump for Diabetics* includes a basic food log to help you record what you eat, what time you eat, and how many grams of carbs your food contains. My hope is that this simple tool makes it just a little bit quicker and easier to manage your diabetes and get on with enjoying your day.

Introduction to Dump Cooking

What is Dump Cooking?

If you're like most people trying to lead a busy life in the modern world, you probably often rely on things like fast food and pizza delivery for dinner. You know eating this way is unhealthy and expensive, yet you can't seem to find the time to get a healthy, home-cooked meal on the table for your family. Many people have simply given up on the idea of cooking because it seems so time consuming and stressful, so you're not alone.

You probably think that the type of person who cooks home-cooked meals for their family everyday has a gourmet kitchen, loads of fancy high end cooking appliances, and tons of time to spend in the kitchen slaving away. What if I told you that you can cook dinner every night, eat a delicious, healthy dinner with your family, and not have the added stress of expensive ingredients, endless prepping, and a sink full of dishes when you're done? Impossible, you say? Not hardly.

Dump cooking is a technique that allows you to simply "dump" a variety of ingredients into a pot, pan, or casserole dish, turn on the heat or pop it in the oven, and turn out delicious healthy meals that the whole family will love. In many cases, you only use one cooking vessel along with a few utensils, so dishes and clean up is practically non-existent. With minimal effort, you'll whip up meals that are super easy, super fast, absolutely delicious, and just right for your diet.

In this book, you'll find dump recipes for low carb dinners, side dishes, and desserts of all kinds. All of them can be prepared with very little effort. For even less effort, plenty of them can be prepared with five ingredients or less. Yes, you can prepare a delicious, low-carb meal with just five ingredients!

DINNERS

Sandwiches

Philly Cheesesteaks

Serves 4

INGREDIENTS:

2 large green bell peppers, sliced into strips

1 medium onion, sliced

8–10 button mushrooms, sliced

2 tablespoons olive oil

1 tablespoon minced garlic

Salt & pepper to taste

8 ounces thin-sliced roast beef, cut into
1 ½-inch strips

4 slices of low-fat provolone or Swiss cheese

4 whole wheat sandwich rolls

DIRECTIONS:

1. Sauté peppers, onion, and mushrooms over medium-high heat in olive oil.
2. Add garlic and season vegetables with salt and pepper. Decrease heat to medium and stir occasionally until onions become translucent.
3. Add roast beef to pan. Sauté for an additional 5–10 minutes.
4. Top with cheese slices and allow to melt.
5. Spoon onto rolls and serve warm.

NUTRITION FACTS

4 Servings

Amount Per Serving	
Calories	358
Total Fat	15 g
Saturated Fat	4 g
Polyunsaturated Fat	0.5 g
Monounsaturated Fat	5 g
Cholesterol	40 mg
Sodium	586 mg
Potassium	81.5 mg
Total Carbohydrates	30 g
Dietary Fiber	4.5 g
Sugars	6.5 g
Protein	27 g

Sloppy Joes

Serves 6

INGREDIENTS:

1 pound lean ground turkey

½ cup chopped onion

½ cup chopped green bell pepper

½ teaspoon garlic powder

2 teaspoons prepared mustard

¾ cup no-salt-added ketchup

1 teaspoon chili powder (optional)

8 whole wheat hamburger buns, split and toasted

Shredded reduced-fat cheddar cheese (optional)

Salt and pepper, to taste

DIRECTIONS:

1. Brown ground turkey in a medium skillet over medium heat. Add onion and green pepper to skillet, and cook until onions are translucent. Drain.

2. Stir in garlic powder, mustard, ketchup, and chili powder (if desired). Simmer on low for 25 minutes.

3. Scoop onto hamburger bun. If desired, sprinkle with reduced-fat cheddar cheese and season with salt and pepper.

NUTRITION FACTS

6 Servings

Amount Per Serving	
Calories	331
Total Fat	8 g
Saturated Fat	2.5 g
Polyunsaturated Fat	1.5 g
Monounsaturated Fat	0 g
Cholesterol	53.5 mg
Sodium	653.5 mg
Potassium	34.5 mg
Total Carbohydrates	44.5 g
Dietary Fiber	6 g
Sugars	3 g
Protein	23g

Teriyaki Turkey Burgers

Serves 4

INGREDIENTS:

1 pound lean ground turkey

2 tablespoons low-sodium soy sauce

1 tablespoon peeled fresh ginger, grated

1 garlic clove, minced

¼ cup chopped green onions

Salt and pepper, to taste

4 whole wheat burger rolls

DIRECTIONS:

1. Combine all ingredients in a bowl.
2. Form into 4 patties.
3. Grill or broil until cooked to desired doneness.
4. Serve on whole wheat rolls.

NUTRITION FACTS

4 Servings

Amount Per Serving	
Calories	339
Total Fat	10 g
Saturated Fat	2.5 g
Polyunsaturated Fat	0 g
Monounsaturated Fat	0 g
Cholesterol	80 mg
Sodium	664 mg
Potassium	24.5 mg
Total Carbohydrates	34.5 g
Dietary Fiber	1 g
Sugars	5 g
Protein	27.5 g

Asian Lettuce Wraps

Serves 4

INGREDIENTS:

1 pound ground chicken or pork

½ cup chopped onion

½ teaspoon garlic powder

½ cup sugar-free Asian dressing

1 cup shredded cabbage

1 head Iceberg lettuce, leaves left in tact

DIRECTIONS:

1. Heat a large skillet over medium heat. Add the beef, onions, and garlic powder, and cook until chicken or pork is no longer pink.
2. Add the dressing and shredded cabbage and cook until cabbage is soft.
3. To serve, spoon into lettuce leaves.

NUTRITION FACTS

4 Servings

Amount Per Serving	
Calories	302
Total Fat	19.5 g
Saturated Fat	3.5 g
Polyunsaturated Fat	0 g
Monounsaturated Fat	0 g
Cholesterol	95 mg
Sodium	338 mg
Potassium	276 mg
Total Carbohydrates	9 g
Dietary Fiber	2.5 g
Sugars	2.5 g
Protein	23 g

Fast and Easy Fajitas

Serves 4

INGREDIENTS:

- 1 pound chicken breast or thigh meat, sliced into strips
- 1 tablespoon fajita seasoning mix
- 1 large onion, sliced
- 2 green bell peppers, seeded and sliced into strips
- 12 corn or low-carb tortillas, warmed

DIRECTIONS:

1. Preheat the oven to 350 degrees F. Put the fajita-seasoning mix and chicken strips in a plastic or paper bag, and shake to coat.
2. In a 9 x 13 inch casserole dish, layer onions, peppers, and seasoned chicken.
3. Bake for 30 minutes. Spoon onto tortillas, roll up, and enjoy.

NUTRITION FACTS

4 Servings

Amount Per Serving	
Calories	266.5
Total Fat	6 g
Saturated Fat	1 g
Polyunsaturated Fat	0.5 g
Monounsaturated Fat	1 g
Cholesterol	70 mg
Sodium	230 mg
Potassium	271 mg
Total Carbohydrates	26.5 g
Dietary Fiber	1.5 g
Sugars	2 g
Protein	29.5 g

Sausage Sloppy Joes

Serves 5

INGREDIENTS:

- 1 pound bulk sausage
- 2 large onions, chopped
- 1 green pepper, chopped
- 1 ½ cups no salt added pasta sauce
- 5 hamburger rolls

DIRECTIONS:

1. Brown sausage, onions, and pepper in a large skillet. Add sauce, cover, and simmer over medium heat for 10–15 minutes. Serve on rolls.

NUTRITION FACTS

5 Servings

Amount Per Serving	
Calories	381.5
Total Fat	20.5 g
Saturated Fat	10.5 g
Polyunsaturated Fat	4.5 g
Monounsaturated Fat	13 g
Cholesterol	68.5 mg
Sodium	1,045.5 mg
Potassium	296 mg
Total Carbohydrates	33.5 g
Dietary Fiber	6.5 g
Sugars	7.5 g
Protein	20 g

Turkey Meatball Subs

Serves 6

INGREDIENTS:

- 1 28-ounce jar pasta sauce
- 1 bag frozen turkey meatballs (about 24 meatballs)
- 6 whole-wheat sub rolls
- 6 slices reduced-fat mozzarella or Swiss cheese

DIRECTIONS:

1. Pour pasta sauce into a large saucepan. Add frozen meatballs and allow to cook over medium-low heat until meatballs are warmed through.
2. Spoon 4 meatballs and sauce onto sub rolls.
3. Add a slice of cheese over each prepared sub and allow it to melt before eating.

NUTRITION FACTS

6 Servings

Amount Per Serving	
Calories	439.5
Total Fat	20 g
Saturated Fat	8 g
Polyunsaturated Fat	2.5 g
Monounsaturated Fat	3.5 g
Cholesterol	46 mg
Sodium	1,211 mg
Potassium	461.5 mg
Total Carbohydrates	41.5 g
Dietary Fiber	6.5 g
Sugars	2 g
Protein	25 g

Chickpea Fritters

Serves 4

INGREDIENTS:

1 15-ounce can chickpeas, drained and rinsed

½ medium onion, chopped

½ teaspoon garlic powder

½ cup whole-wheat flour

1 egg, beaten

1 teaspoon olive oil

DIRECTIONS:

1. Add chickpeas and onions to a food processor and pulse until a paste forms.

2. Pulse in garlic powder, flour, and egg. Remove and use hands to shape mixture into patties.

3. Fry patties in olive oil over medium-high heat until golden brown.

NUTRITION FACTS

4 Servings

Amount Per Serving	
Calories	194
Total Fat	3.5 g
Saturated Fat	0.5 g
Polyunsaturated Fat	0.5 g
Monounsaturated Fat	1.5 g
Cholesterol	46.5 mg
Sodium	298 mg
Potassium	39 mg
Total Carbohydrates	30.3 g
Dietary Fiber	8 g
Sugars	1 g
Protein	10 g

Casseroles

Taco Casserole

Serves 6

INGREDIENTS:

1 ½ cups ground beef

1 can refried beans

1 ½ teaspoons paprika

1 teaspoon chili powder

½ teaspoon oregano

½ teaspoon garlic powder

4 cups crushed low-salt baked tortilla chips

1 cup shredded low-fat Mexican blend cheese

DIRECTIONS:

1. Preheat oven to 350 degrees F.
2. Brown beef in a pan over medium-high heat and cook until no longer pink. Drain.
3. Mix in beans and seasonings.
4. Spray a large casserole dish with cooking spray.
5. Spread the seasoned beef into the casserole dish. Add a layer of tortilla chips and sprinkle on the cheese.
6. Bake for 20 minutes or until cheese is bubbly.

NUTRITION FACTS

6 Servings

Amount Per Serving	
Calories	449.5
Total Fat	24.5 g
Saturated Fat	8 g
Polyunsaturated Fat	0.5 g
Monounsaturated Fat	5.5 g
Cholesterol	59 mg
Sodium	595 mg
Potassium	397.5 mg
Total Carbohydrates	32.5 g
Dietary Fiber	7 g
Sugars	0.5 g
Protein	22 g

Skillet Lasagna

Serves 4–6

INGREDIENTS:

1 pound lean ground beef

1 tablespoon garlic powder

1 tablespoon onion powder

1 teaspoon dried basil

2 tablespoons dried oregano

1 tablespoon dried parsley

1 cup water

1 cup whole-grain pasta, such as penne

1 (28-ounce) jar low-sodium pasta sauce

½ cup low-fat ricotta cheese

1 cup shredded low-fat mozzarella cheese

DIRECTIONS:

1. Heat a medium skillet over medium heat. Add the ground beef and seasonings. Cook until beef is no longer pink.

2. Add the water and pasta. Bring to a boil and reduce heat to medium low. Cover and cook for 10 minutes, until pasta is tender.

3. Add the sauce, stir in cheeses, and heat through. Serve.

NUTRITION FACTS

6 Servings

Amount Per Serving	
Calories	475.5
Total Fat	22 g
Saturated Fat	9.5 g
Polyunsaturated Fat	1 g
Monounsaturated Fat	7.5 g
Cholesterol	73 mg
Sodium	216.5 mg
Potassium	290 mg
Total Carbohydrates	42 g
Dietary Fiber	5 g
Sugars	10.5 g
Protein	28.5 g

Chicken Nacho Bake

Serves 6

INGREDIENTS:

2 cups chopped or shredded chicken, cooked

2 cups whole-grain tortilla chips

1 ½ cups shredded low-fat Mexican-style cheese

½ cup reduced-fat sour cream

¼ cup chopped green onions

DIRECTIONS:

1. Preheat oven to 350 degrees F. Layer the chicken, tortilla chips, and cheese in a 9 x 13 inch casserole dish.

2. Bake for 10 minutes, or until cheese is melted. Remove from oven and allow to cool slightly.

3. Top with sour cream and green onions and serve.

NUTRITION FACTS

6 Servings

Amount Per Serving	
Calories	249
Total Fat	13 g
Saturated Fat	6 g
Polyunsaturated Fat	0.5 g
Monounsaturated Fat	1.5 g
Cholesterol	58 mg
Sodium	312 mg
Potassium	137.5 mg
Total Carbohydrates	10 g
Dietary Fiber	1.5 g
Sugars	1 g
Protein	22 g

Oven Quesadillas

Serves 4

INGREDIENTS:

2 cups chopped or shredded chicken, cooked

1 16-ounce jar salsa

1 cup shredded low-fat Mexican-style cheese

8 whole-wheat tortillas

DIRECTIONS:

1. Preheat oven to 350 degrees F.
2. Place the chicken in a plastic bag. Pour in salsa and shake to coat.
3. Lay half the tortillas on a sheet pan coated with cooking spray. Spread the chicken mixture over the tortillas. Sprinkle with cheese. Top with remaining tortillas.
4. Bake for 10 minutes until cheese is melted and tops of tortillas are lightly browned and crisp.

NUTRITION FACTS

4 Servings

Amount Per Serving	
Calories	465
Total Fat	14 g
Saturated Fat	6.5 g
Polyunsaturated Fat	0.5 g
Monounsaturated Fat	1 g
Cholesterol	67.5 mg
Sodium	1,116.5 mg
Potassium	303 mg
Total Carbohydrates	48 g
Dietary Fiber	7 g
Sugars	4 g
Protein	35 g

Meatball Marinara Bake

Serves 6

INGREDIENTS:

1 bag frozen meatballs

½ pound cooked whole-grain pasta (such as penne)

3 cups low sodium pasta sauce

2 cups low-fat shredded mozzarella cheese

DIRECTIONS:

1. Preheat oven to 350 degrees F. Spray a 9 x 13 inch casserole dish with cooking spray.

2. Layer the meatballs, pasta, and sauce with half of the cheese.

3. Cover with foil and bake for 45 minutes, until meatballs are heated through.

4. Uncover, top with remaining cheese, and bake for 10 more minutes or until cheese is bubbly.

NUTRITION FACTS

6 Servings

Amount Per Serving	
Calories	525.5
Total Fat	21.5 g
Saturated Fat	8.5 g
Polyunsaturated Fat	0 g
Monounsaturated Fat	0 g
Cholesterol	59 mg
Sodium	589 mg
Potassium	0 mg
Total Carbohydrates	54 g
Dietary Fiber	7 g
Sugars	10 g
Protein	30.5 g

Gumbo Casserole

Serves 6

INGREDIENTS:

- 2 cans low-sodium condensed cream of chicken soup
- 1 cup water
- 1 teaspoon onion power
- ½ teaspoon Cajun seasoning
- ½ teaspoon garlic powder
- 1 cup frozen okra
- ¾ cup brown rice, uncooked
- 1 cup extra-lean low-sodium ham, cooked and diced
- ½ pound peeled and deveined cocktail shrimp

DIRECTIONS:

1. Preheat oven to 350 degrees F. Mix together first 6 ingredients in a large bowl. Add in rice, ham, and shrimp. Stir. Empty into a casserole dish.
2. Bake for 30–35 minutes, until rice is tender.

NUTRITION FACTS

6 Servings

Amount Per Serving	
Calories	234.5
Total Fat	9.5 g
Saturated Fat	3 g
Polyunsaturated Fat	1g
Monounsaturated Fat	2.5 g
Cholesterol	68.5 mg
Sodium	1,167 mg
Potassium	153 mg
Total Carbohydrates	19 g
Dietary Fiber	1.5 g
Sugars	1.5 g
Protein	22 g

Turkey Noodle Casserole

Serves 8

INGREDIENTS:

- 2 cans low-sodium cream of mushroom soup
- 1 cup skim milk
- 2 cups frozen peas
- 2 cups shredded or chopped turkey, cooked
- 2 cups low-sodium egg white noodles, cooked
- 1 tablespoon bread crumbs
- 1 tablespoon olive oil

DIRECTIONS:

1. Preheat oven to 350 degrees F.
2. Combine the soup, milk, peas, turkey, and noodles in a 3-quart casserole dish.
3. Sprinkle with bread crumbs and drizzle with oil.
4. Bake for 30–35 minutes until top is browned and casserole is hot and bubbly.

NUTRITION FACTS

8 Servings

Amount Per Serving	
Calories	217.5
Total Fat	6 g
Saturated Fat	1.5 g
Polyunsaturated Fat	1.5 g
Monounsaturated Fat	2 g
Cholesterol	39 mg
Sodium	564 mg
Potassium	662.5 mg
Total Carbohydrates	24 g
Dietary Fiber	3 g
Sugars	5.5 g
Protein	16 g

Mushroom Beef Bake

Serves 4–6

INGREDIENTS:

1 can low-sodium cream of mushroom soup

1 (8-ounce) package low fat cream cheese, softened

¼ cup skim milk

½ envelope low sodium onion soup mix

1 ½ pounds lean ground beef, cooked

1 cup mushrooms, sliced

DIRECTIONS:

1. Preheat oven to 375 degrees F.
2. Spray a 2-quart casserole dish with nonstick spray.
3. Mix soup, cream cheese, milk, and onion soup mix in casserole until smooth.
4. Add ground beef and mushrooms and stir to blend.
5. Bake for 30 minutes or until hot and bubbly.

NUTRITION FACTS

6 Servings

Amount Per Serving	
Calories	455
Total Fat	32 g
Saturated Fat	14.5 g
Polyunsaturated Fat	2 g
Monounsaturated Fat	12.5 g
Cholesterol	111 mg
Sodium	514.5 mg
Potassium	702 mg
Total Carbohydrates	12.5 g
Dietary Fiber	1 g
Sugars	2.5 g
Protein	26 g

Amazingly Easy Enchiladas

Serves 4

INGREDIENTS:

1 pound ground beef

1 16-ounce jar salsa

1 cup low-fat shredded mozzarella cheese

12 corn or low-carb tortillas

DIRECTIONS:

1. Preheat oven to 350 degrees F.
2. Heat a skillet over medium heat and add the beef. When cooked through, stir in half the salsa and half the cheese. Stir until heated and cheese is melted.
3. Pour half of the remaining salsa in the bottom of a large casserole dish.
4. Spoon some of the beef onto a tortilla and fold the sides up. Flip the tortilla over and lay the tortilla seam side down in the casserole dish. Repeat for all tortillas. Top with remaining salsa and cheese.
5. Bake for 15–20 minutes, until cheese is melted.

NUTRITION FACTS

4 Servings

Amount Per Serving	
Calories	341
Total Fat	21g
Saturated Fat	8.5 g
Polyunsaturated Fat	0.5 g
Monounsaturated Fat	7 g
Cholesterol	66.5 mg
Sodium	602 mg
Potassium	381 mg
Total Carbohydrates	18 g
Dietary Fiber	1.5 g
Sugars	0 g
Protein	21 g

Burger Casserole

Serves 8

INGREDIENTS:

1 pound lean ground beef

½ teaspoon onion powder

¼ teaspoon garlic powder

Pinch salt and pepper

½ cup no-salt-added ketchup

¼ cup yellow mustard

4 medium sweet potatoes, peeled and cubed

1 can sliced carrots, drained and rinsed

2 tablespoons water

4 slices reduced-fat, reduced-sodium
    American cheese

DIRECTIONS:

1. Preheat oven to 350 degrees F. Lay ground
   beef in greased 9-inch square pan. Sprinkle
   with a mixture of onion powder, garlic
   powder, salt, and pepper.

2. Mix together ketchup and mustard and pour
   over seasoned beef. Layer on potatoes and
   carrots. Sprinkle with water.

3. Cover with foil and bake 1 ½ hours. Add
   cheese on top and serve warm.

NUTRITION FACTS

8 Servings

Amount Per Serving	
Calories	257.5
Total Fat	13.5 g
Saturated Fat	5.5 g
Polyunsaturated Fat	0.5 g
Monounsaturated Fat	5.5 g
Cholesterol	47.5 mg
Sodium	446.5 mg
Potassium	338 mg
Total Carbohydrates	20 g
Dietary Fiber	3 g
Sugars	2.5 g
Protein	13.5 g

Baked Reuben on Rye Casserole

Serves 10

INGREDIENTS:

- 1 cup sugar-free Thousand Island dressing
- 1 cup fat-free sour cream
- 10 slices dark rye bread, cubed
- 1 14.5 ounce can shredded sauerkraut, drained and rinsed
- ¾ pound corned beef, trimmed of fat and chopped
- 1 cup fat-free shredded Swiss cheese

DIRECTIONS:

1. Preheat oven to 350 degrees F. Line bottom of a 9 x 13 inch casserole dish with most of the bread cubes (reserve some for topping).
2. Top with sauerkraut, corned beef, dressing, cheese, and remaining bread cubes.
3. Cover with foil and bake for 15 minutes. Uncover and bake 10 more minutes or until bubbly.

NUTRITION FACTS

10 Servings

Amount Per Serving	
Calories	265.5
Total Fat	13.5 g
Saturated Fat	5.5 g
Polyunsaturated Fat	0 g
Monounsaturated Fat	0.5 g
Cholesterol	42.5 mg
Sodium	1,088 mg
Potassium	127 mg
Total Carbohydrates	20.5 g
Dietary Fiber	2 g
Sugars	3.5 g
Protein	15 g

Turkey Sausage Bake

Serves 6

INGREDIENTS:

- ¾ pound ground turkey
- ¼ cup chopped onions
- 1 cup fat-free cottage cheese
- 1 cup fat-free milk
- 1 10.75-ounce can low sodium cream of mushroom soup
- 2 cups egg white noodles, cooked
- 1 cup fat-free shredded cheddar cheese

DIRECTIONS:

1. Preheat oven to 350 degrees F. Grease a 2-quart casserole dish.
2. Brown turkey and onion in a skillet. Add cottage cheese, milk, and soup to skillet and mix. Add in noodles.
3. Pour skillet contents into casserole dish and bake uncovered for 45 minutes or until bubbly and browned.

NUTRITION FACTS

6 Servings

Amount Per Serving	
Calories	272
Total Fat	11.5 g
Saturated Fat	4.5 g
Polyunsaturated Fat	2 g
Monounsaturated Fat	2.5 g
Cholesterol	74 mg
Sodium	551 mg
Potassium	413.5 mg
Total Carbohydrates	17.5 g
Dietary Fiber	1 g
Sugars	4 g
Protein	24.5 g

Cornflake Chicken Casserole

Serves: 6

INGREDIENTS:

3 cups cooked chicken breast, cubed

1 10.75-ounce can, reduced-sodium condensed
    cream of chicken soup

¼ cup low-fat milk

1 cup green pepper, chopped

¼ cup green onions, sliced

¼ teaspoon pepper

¼ cup crushed cornflakes

DIRECTIONS:

1. Preheat oven to 400 degrees F.

2. Add all ingredients, except cornflakes, to
   a 2-quart casserole dish coated with olive
   oil cooking spray. Stir gently until well
   combined. Sprinkle cornflakes on top.

3. Bake, uncovered, for 30 minutes.

NUTRITION FACTS

6 Servings

Amount Per Serving	
Calories	174.5
Total Fat	6 g
Saturated Fat	2 g
Polyunsaturated Fat	1 g
Monounsaturated Fat	2 g
Cholesterol	58 mg
Sodium	384.5 mg
Potassium	267 mg
Total Carbohydrates	8 g
Dietary Fiber	0.5 g
Sugars	1.5 g
Protein	21 g

Ginger Chicken Casserole

Serves: 6

INGREDIENTS:

1 10.75-ounce can reduced-sodium cream of chicken soup

1 6-ounce container of plain, low-fat yogurt

3 cups chicken breast, cooked and cubed

2 ribs celery, chopped

¼ cup green onions, chopped

½ teaspoon ground ginger

Dash of salt and pepper

DIRECTIONS:

1. Preheat oven to 400 degrees F. Gently mix soup and yogurt together in a 9 x 9 inch baking dish coated in olive oil cooking spray.
2. Add remaining ingredients and stir gently.
3. Bake 30–35 minutes, or until heated through.

NUTRITION FACTS

6 Servings

Amount Per Serving	
Calories	182
Total Fat	6.5 g
Saturated Fat	2 g
Polyunsaturated Fat	1.5 g
Monounsaturated Fat	2.5 g
Cholesterol	58.5 mg
Sodium	476 mg
Potassium	356 mg
Total Carbohydrates	8 g
Dietary Fiber	0.5 g
Sugars	2 g
Protein	22.5 g

Chicken and Corn Bread Casserole

Serves 8

INGREDIENTS:

2 eggs, lightly beaten

1 box corn muffin mix

3 cups low-sodium chicken broth, warmed

1 10.75-ounce can low-sodium condensed cream of chicken soup

4 cups cubed chicken breast, cooked

1 8-ounce can whole kernel corn, drained and rinsed

Dash of salt and pepper

DIRECTIONS:

1. Preheat oven to 375 degrees F.
2. Combine all ingredients in a 13 x 9 inch baking dish coated with olive oil cooking spray.
3. Cover and bake for 30 minutes. Uncover and bake 10–15 minutes longer, or until warmed through.

NUTRITION FACTS

8 Servings

Amount Per Serving	
Calories	255.5
Total Fat	8 g
Saturated Fat	2 g
Polyunsaturated Fat	1.5 g
Monounsaturated Fat	2.5 g
Cholesterol	109.5 mg
Sodium	812 mg
Potassium	369.5 mg
Total Carbohydrates	21 g
Dietary Fiber	0.5 g
Sugars	5 g
Protein	24.5 g

Italian Zucchini Bake

Serves 8

INGREDIENTS:

1 ½ pounds lean ground pork

1 medium onion, chopped

½ teaspoon garlic powder

½ teaspoon Italian seasoning

1 ½ pounds zucchini, peeled and sliced

½ cup low-fat shredded mozzarella cheese

1 can low-sodium cream of mushroom soup

¾ cup low-fat milk

DIRECTIONS:

1. In a skillet over medium-high heat, add pork, onion, and seasonings and cook until pork is no longer pink in the middle. Remove pork from the skillet.

2. Add zucchini to skillet and cook until soft.

3. In the bottom of a 13 x 9 inch baking dish, arrange half of sausage mixture, top with half of zucchini, then layer on half of cheese. Repeat. Combine soup and milk and pour over the top.

4. Bake at 350 degrees F for 30 minutes.

NUTRITION FACTS

8 Servings

Amount Per Serving	
Calories	253.5
Total Fat	5 g
Saturated Fat	6 g
Polyunsaturated Fat	1.5 g
Monounsaturated Fat	6 g
Cholesterol	64 mg
Sodium	276 mg
Potassium	646.5 mg
Total Carbohydrates	9.5 g
Dietary Fiber	2 g
Sugars	3 g
Protein	19 g

Zucchini Eggplant Casserole

Serves 8

INGREDIENTS:

2 tablespoons olive oil

1 medium eggplant, diced

1 small zucchini, finely diced

½ cup water

10 ounces baby spinach

1 ½ cups prepared low-sodium pasta sauce

½ cup chopped fresh basil

1 ½ cups shredded part-skim mozzarella, divided

DIRECTIONS

1. Preheat oven to 450 degrees F. Coat a 13 x 9 inch baking dish with olive oil cooking spray.

2. In a skillet over medium-high heat, cook eggplant and zucchini until softened and slightly brown. Add water and spinach; cover and cook 3 minutes. Add in pasta sauce and basil.

3. Pour into baking dish and sprinkle with cheese. Bake 15 minutes, or until cheese is bubbly.

NUTRITION FACTS

8 Servings

Amount Per Serving	
Calories	131.5
Total Fat	7.5 g
Saturated Fat	3 g
Polyunsaturated Fat	0.5 g
Monounsaturated Fat	2.5 g
Cholesterol	11.5 mg
Sodium	398.5 mg
Potassium	517.5 mg
Total Carbohydrates	9 g
Dietary Fiber	3.5 g
Sugars	2 g
Protein	8.5 g

In a Hurry Hashbrown Casserole

Serves 10

INGREDIENTS:

- 1 10.75-ounce can reduced-sodium condensed cream of chicken soup
- 1 cup reduced-fat cheddar cheese, shredded
- ⅔ cup reduced-fat sour cream
- 1 bag frozen shredded hash brown potatoes, thawed
- 2 cups cooked ham, cubed
- 1 small onion, chopped
- Dash salt and pepper

DIRECTIONS:

1. Preheat oven to 350 degrees F.
2. Mix first 3 ingredients together in a 13 x 9 inch baking dish coated with olive oil cooking spray. Add in remaining ingredients and stir gently.
3. Bake for 40 minutes or until heated through.

NUTRITION FACTS

10 Servings

Amount Per Serving	
Calories	151
Total Fat	9 g
Saturated Fat	4 g
Polyunsaturated Fat	0.5 g
Monounsaturated Fat	2.5 g
Cholesterol	32 mg
Sodium	665 mg
Potassium	136 mg
Total Carbohydrates	8.5 g
Dietary Fiber	0 g
Sugars	0 g
Protein	9.5 g

Cream Corn Casserole

Serves 8

INGREDIENTS:

¼ cup egg substitute

¼ cup butter, melted

1 can no-salt-added whole-kernel corn, drained and rinsed

1 can no-salt-added cream-style corn

1 8-ounce container plain, fat-free yogurt

1 8.5-ounce package corn bread mix

2 cups cooked chicken, cubed

DIRECTIONS:

1. Preheat oven to 350 degrees F.
2. In a 9 x 9 inch baking dish coated with olive oil cooking spray, combine first 5 ingredients. Add in corn muffin mix and chicken. Bake for 40–45 minutes.

NUTRITION FACTS

8 Servings

Amount Per Serving	
Calories	301.5
Total Fat	8.5 g
Saturated Fat	4 g
Polyunsaturated Fat	0.5 g
Monounsaturated Fat	2.5 g
Cholesterol	42.5 mg
Sodium	408 mg
Potassium	290 mg
Total Carbohydrates	34 g
Dietary Fiber	1 g
Sugars	4 g
Protein	15 g

Chili Dog Casserole

Serves 4–6

INGREDIENTS:

2 15-ounce cans chili with beans

6 hot dogs

8 6-inch corn or whole-wheat tortillas

½ cup shredded reduced-fat cheddar cheese

DIRECTIONS:

1. Heat oven to 400 degrees F.
2. Spread chili on bottom of 11 x 7 inch baking dish.
3. Place one hot dog on each tortilla; roll it up. Place the seam-side down on top of the chili.
4. Spray lightly with olive oil cooking spray to help brown tortillas.
5. Bake 15 minutes or until hot dogs are heated through and tortillas are browned.
6. Sprinkle with cheese and bake until cheese is melted, about 5 more minutes.

NUTRITION FACTS

6 Servings

Amount Per Serving	
Calories	383
Total Fat	22.5 g
Saturated Fat	9 g
Polyunsaturated Fat	2 g
Monounsaturated Fat	9.5 g
Cholesterol	51 mg
Sodium	1,264.5 mg
Potassium	607 mg
Total Carbohydrate	31.5 g
Dietary Fiber	9 g
Sugars	2 g
Protein	17 g

Pizza Muffins

Serves 10

INGREDIENTS:

1 7.5-ounce tube low-fat refrigerated biscuits

¾ pound lean ground beef

1 6-ounce can tomato paste

1 tablespoon chopped onion

1 teaspoon Italian seasoning

½ cup fat-free shredded mozzarella cheese

DIRECTIONS:

1. Preheat oven to 400 degrees F. Press biscuits into bottom and sides of greased muffin pan.

2. Brown beef over medium heat in a large skillet. Add tomato paste, onion, and seasoning. Dump into biscuit "cups" and sprinkle with cheese.

3. Bake for 12–15 minutes, until cheese is hot and bubbly.

NUTRITION FACTS

10 Servings

Amount Per Serving	
Calories	256
Total Fat	13 g
Saturated Fat	6 g
Polyunsaturated Fat	0.5 g
Monounsaturated Fat	3 g
Cholesterol	28.5 mg
Sodium	671.5 mg
Potassium	262.5 mg
Total Carbohydrates	24 g
Dietary Fiber	1.5 g
Sugars	6 g
Protein	8.5 g

Egg and Veggie Bake

Serves: 6

INGREDIENTS:

2 cups egg substitute

1 cup shredded reduced-fat mozzarella cheese

1 teaspoon Italian seasoning

2 teaspoons olive oil

¼ cup onion, chopped

1 cup mushrooms, sliced

½ bag fresh spinach, steamed

DIRECTIONS:

1. Preheat oven to 350 degrees F.

2. Whisk together egg substitute, cheese, and Italian seasoning in a 9 x 9 inch baking dish coated in olive oil spray.

3. In a large skillet, cook onions and mushrooms in oil over medium heat. Add spinach and cook for 2–3 minutes, or until wilted. Add veggies to egg mixture and stir gently. Bake 30 to 35 minutes, or until eggs are set in center.

NUTRITION FACTS

6 Servings

Amount Per Serving	
Calories	121.5
Total Fat	5 g
Saturated Fat	2 g
Polyunsaturated Fat	0 g
Monounsaturated Fat	1 g
Cholesterol	10 mg
Sodium	293 mg
Potassium	304 mg
Total Carbohydrates	3.5 g
Dietary Fiber	1 g
Sugars	0.5 g
Protein	15.5 g

Chicken and Poultry

Crispy Pesto Chicken Bake

Serves 4

INGREDIENTS:

4 bone-in chicken leg quarters, skin removed

½ cup prepared pesto

1 cup Panko bread crumbs

½ cup low-fat shredded mozzarella cheese

DIRECTIONS:

1. Preheat oven to 350 degrees F.
2. Coat the chicken in the pesto. Put the breadcrumbs in a shallow pan.
3. Dredge the chicken in the breadcrumbs. Lay on a baking sheet.
4. Bake for 25–30 minutes until chicken is cooked through. Remove from oven and top with the cheese. Bake for 5 minutes until cheese is melted and serve.

NUTRITION FACTS

4 Servings

Amount Per Serving	
Calories	406
Total Fat	23 g
Saturated Fat	5.5 g
Polyunsaturated Fat	1 g
Monounsaturated Fat	1.5 g
Cholesterol	119 mg
Sodium	497 mg
Potassium	297.5 mg
Total Carbohydrate	13.5 g
Dietary Fiber	1 g
Sugars	1.5 g
Protein	34 g

Balsamic Chicken Breasts

Serves 4

INGREDIENTS:

- 4 boneless, skinless chicken breasts
- 1 bunch basil leaves
- 4 slices low-fat mozzarella cheese
- 4 sundried tomatoes
- 4 tablespoons sugar-free Balsamic Vinaigrette salad dressing

DIRECTIONS:

1. Preheat oven to 350 degrees F.
2. Make a cut in the side of each chicken breast. Insert 1 or 2 basil leaves, a slice of cheese, and a sundried tomato into each.
3. Lay the chicken breasts on a baking sheet and brush each with a tablespoon of dressing.
4. Bake 30–45 minutes until chicken is cooked through.

NUTRITION FACTS

4 Servings

Amount Per Serving	
Total Calories	240
Total Fat	9 g
Saturated Fat	4 g
Polyunsaturated Fat	1 g
Monounsaturated Fat	2 g
Cholesterol	88 mg
Sodium	359 mg
Potassium	0 mg
Carbohydrate	2 g
Dietary Fiber	0 g
Total Sugars	1 g
Added Sugars	0 g
Protein	34 g

Honey Dijon Skillet Chicken

Serves 4

INGREDIENTS:

¾ pound red potatoes, quartered

1 cup sugar-free honey mustard salad dressing

1 tablespoon chopped onion

4 boneless, skinless chicken breasts

DIRECTIONS:

1. Preheat oven to 350 degrees F. Spray a baking sheet with cooking spray.
2. Toss chicken, potatoes, and onion with dressing (in a bag or bowl). Lay marinated ingredients on the baking sheet.
3. Bake for 30–35 minutes, or until chicken is cooked through.

NUTRITION FACTS

4 Servings

Amount Per Serving	
Calories	493
Total Fat	26.5 g
Saturated Fat	5g
Polyunsaturated Fat	0 g
Monounsaturated Fat	0 g
Cholesterol	90 mg
Sodium	711.5 mg
Potassium	546 mg
Total Carbohydrates	34 g
Dietary Fiber	3 g
Sugars	25.5 g
Protein	24.5 g

Stir-Fry Italian Chicken

Serves 4–6

INGREDIENTS:

¼ cup sugar-free Italian dressing

2 boneless, skinless chicken breasts, cubed

1 bag frozen vegetables

¼ cup reduced fat grated Parmesan cheese

DIRECTIONS:

1. Heat a large skillet over medium heat. Add the dressing and the chicken and cook until chicken is browned on all sides.

2. Add the vegetables and continue cooking until tender. Stir in the cheese.

NUTRITION FACTS

4 Servings

Amount Per Serving	
Calories	138
Total Fat	4 g
Saturated Fat	1.5 g
Polyunsaturated Fat	0 g
Monounsaturated Fat	0.5 g
Cholesterol	39 mg
Sodium	501.5 mg
Potassium	156 mg
Total Carbohydrates	10 g
Dietary Fiber	3 g
Sugars	0 g
Protein	15.5 g

Skillet Turkey Sausage

Serves 6

INGREDIENTS:

2 teaspoons olive oil

1 medium onion, diced

1 red bell pepper, seeded and diced

1 clove garlic, minced

8 ounces turkey kielbasa, diced

1 cup low-sodium, fat-free chicken broth

¼ teaspoon crushed red pepper flakes
(or to taste)

¼ teaspoon ground black pepper

1 15.5-oz can black-eyed peas, drained
and rinsed

DIRECTIONS:

1. Add oil to a large skillet. Sauté onion, bell
    pepper and garlic in oil for 5 minutes over
    medium heat. Add kielbasa to skillet and
    sauté for an additional 3 minutes.

2. Add broth, red pepper flakes, ground black
    pepper, and black-eyed peas. Bring to a boil
    then reduce to a simmer. Simmer for
    7 minutes.

NUTRITION FACTS

6 Servings

Amount Per Serving	
Calories	141.5
Total Fat	5 g
Saturated Fat	0 g
Polyunsaturated Fat	0 g
Monounsaturated Fat	1 g
Cholesterol	20 mg
Sodium	444.5 mg
Potassium	89.5 mg
Total Carbohydrates	16.5 g
Dietary Fiber	4 g
Sugars	3 g
Protein	8.5 g

Sweet Potato Chicken Bake

Serves 4

INGREDIENTS:

1 tablespoon olive or vegetable oil cooking spray

2 sweet potatoes, peeled and cubed

1 onion, cut into wedges

½ packet Ranch dressing seasoning

4 boneless skinless chicken breasts

DIRECTIONS:

1. Preheat oven to 350 degrees F. Spray a baking sheet with cooking spray.

2. Toss all ingredients in a large bowl or plastic bag. Once everything is coated, remove from the bag and lay in an even layer on the baking sheet.

3. Bake for 30–35 minutes, until chicken is cooked through and sweet potatoes are tender.

NUTRITION FACTS

4 Servings

Amount Per Serving	
Calories	232
Total Fat	6 g
Saturated Fat	1.5 g
Polyunsaturated Fat	0.5 g
Monounsaturated Fat	2.5 g
Cholesterol	70 mg
Sodium	453 mg
Potassium	176 mg
Total Carbohydrates	20 g
Dietary Fiber	2.5 g
Sugars	0 g
Protein	23.5 g

Orange Chicken Bake

Serves 4

INGREDIENTS:

4 boneless skinless chicken breasts

¼ teaspoon paprika

Dash of salt

Dash of pepper

¼ cup sugar-free orange marmalade

2 cups cooked brown rice or couscous

DIRECTIONS:

1. Preheat oven to 350 degrees F. Place chicken breasts on a foil-lined baking sheet. Season with paprika, salt, and pepper.
2. Add a heaping spoonful of marmalade to the top of each chicken breast.
3. Bake for 35–45 minutes, or until chicken is cooked through. Serve over brown rice.

NUTRITION FACTS

4 Servings

Amount Per Serving	
Calories	239
Total Fat	3.5 g
Saturated Fat	1.5 g
Polyunsaturated Fat	0 g
Monounsaturated Fat	0 g
Cholesterol	70 mg
Sodium	390 mg
Potassium	77 mg
Total Carbohydrates	28.5 g
Dietary Fiber	2 g
Sugars	0 g
Protein	24.5 g

Apricot Chicken Pan Roast

Serves 4

INGREDIENTS:

3 boneless, skinless chicken breasts, cubed

1 bag frozen cauliflower florets

1 tablespoon vegetable or olive oil

¼ cup sugar-free apricot jam

DIRECTIONS:

1. Preheat oven to 400 degrees F. Spray a baking sheet with olive oil cooking spray.

2. Add all ingredients to a freezer bag and shake until well coated.

3. Lay on prepared baking sheet in a single layer and roast 30–35 minutes until chicken is cooked through and cauliflower is tender.

NUTRITION FACTS

4 Servings

Amount Per Serving	
Calories	147
Total Fat	5.5 g
Saturated Fat	1 g
Polyunsaturated Fat	0.5 g
Monounsaturated Fat	2.5 g
Cholesterol	52.5 mg
Sodium	278.5 mg
Potassium	125 mg
Total Carbohydrates	8 g
Dietary Fiber	5.5 g
Sugars	1 g
Protein	18 g

Quick and Easy Turkey Meatloaf

Serves 6–8

INGREDIENTS:

1 ½ pounds ground turkey or beef

1 cup water

1 egg

1 box low sodium stuffing mix

DIRECTIONS:

1. Preheat oven to 350 degrees F.
2. Spray 9 x 13 inch baking pan with olive oil cooking spray.
3. Break meat apart into chunks and drop in pan. Add egg to water and whisk with a fork.
4. Add stuffing mix and egg water to pan. Blend together with hands or a large spatula. Form into a loaf in the center of the pan.
5. Bake for 45 minutes.

NUTRITION FACTS

6 Servings

Amount Per Serving	
Calories	282
Total Fat	10 g
Saturated Fat	3 g
Polyunsaturated Fat	0 g
Monounsaturated Fat	0.5 g
Cholesterol	111 mg
Sodium	347 mg
Potassium	11.5 mg
Total Carbohydrates	22 g
Dietary Fiber	0 g
Sugars	2 g
Protein	26 g

Roasted Chicken and Veggies

Serves 4–6

INGREDIENTS:

2 pounds bone-in chicken pieces

½ pound baby carrots

1 onion, sliced

3 medium sweet potatoes, peeled and cubed

1 tablespoon olive oil or vegetable oil

2 teaspoons dried thyme

Pinch of salt and pepper

DIRECTIONS:

1. Preheat oven to 375 degrees F. Spray a 9 x 13 inch casserole dish with olive oil cooking spray.
2. Lay the chicken and vegetables in prepared dish. Drizzle with oil and sprinkle with thyme, salt, and pepper.
3. Bake for 1 hour and check the chicken for doneness. Roast until chicken is cooked through and vegetables are tender.

NUTRITION FACTS

4 Servings

Amount Per Serving	
Calories	213.5
Total Fat	4.5 g
Saturated Fat	0.5 g
Polyunsaturated Fat	1 g
Monounsaturated Fat	3 g
Cholesterol	17 mg
Sodium	109.5 mg
Potassium	652.5 mg
Total Carbohydrates	37 g
Dietary Fiber	6.5 g
Sugars	5g
Protein	7 g

Easy-Peasy Chicken and Peas

Serves 4

INGREDIENTS:

- 4 boneless, skinless chicken breasts, cut into quarters
- 1 cup uncooked brown rice (not instant)
- 1 can low-sodium cream soup (chicken, mushroom, or celery)
- 2 cups hot water
- 2 cups frozen peas

DIRECTIONS:

1. Preheat oven to 375 degrees F.
2. Spray a lidded 2-quart casserole dish with olive oil cooking spray.
3. Mix together rice, soup, water, and peas in casserole dish.
4. Add chicken pieces and stir together.
5. Cover and bake 1 hour until rice has absorbed water and chicken is cooked through.

NUTRITION FACTS

4 Servings

Amount Per Serving	
Calories	354.5
Total Fat	6.5 g
Saturated Fat	2.5 g
Polyunsaturated Fat	1 g
Monounsaturated Fat	0.5 g
Cholesterol	75 mg
Sodium	901.5 mg
Potassium	614.5 mg
Total Carbohydrates	43.5 g
Dietary Fiber	6 g
Sugars	6 g
Protein	29 g

Chicken Milanese

Serves 6

INGREDIENTS:

½ cup sugar-free or light mayonnaise

1 teaspoon garlic powder

6 boneless, skinless chicken breasts

1 cup Panko crumbs

2 tablespoons dried parsley

2 tablespoons vegetable oil

1 bag fresh spinach

DIRECTIONS:

1. Combine the mayo with the garlic powder in a bowl and coat the chicken breasts with the mixture.

2. Combine the Panko crumbs and the parsley in a shallow dish. Dredge the chicken in the crumbs until thoroughly coated.

3. Heat the oil in a medium skillet. Cook the chicken until browned and crispy on both sides. Add spinach to skillet. Cook 3–5 minutes until spinach is soft and wilted.

NUTRITION FACTS

6 Servings

Amount Per Serving	
Calories	207.5
Total Fat	7.5 g
Saturated Fat	4.5 g
Polyunsaturated Fat	0 g
Monounsaturated Fat	0g
Cholesterol	70 mg
Sodium	400.5 mg
Potassium	264 mg
Total Carbohydrates	10.5 g
Dietary Fiber	1.5 g
Sugars	1 g
Protein	24.5 g

Baked Chicken Cordon Bleu

Serves 6

INGREDIENTS:

- 6 boneless, skinless chicken breasts
- 6 slices extra-lean low-sodium cooked ham
- 6 slices low fat Swiss cheese
- 1 can low-sodium condensed cream of chicken soup
- 1 tablespoon Dijon mustard

DIRECTIONS:

1. Preheat the oven to 350 degrees F.
2. Lay the chicken breasts in a baking dish. Lay a slice of ham and Swiss cheese on each piece.
3. Combine the soup with the mustard, and pour the mixture over the chicken. Cover dish with foil.
4. Bake for 30–35 minutes until chicken is cooked through.

NUTRITION FACTS

6 Servings

Amount Per Serving	
Calories	287
Total Fat	9.5 g
Saturated Fat	4 g
Polyunsaturated Fat	0.5 g
Monounsaturated Fat	1.5 g
Cholesterol	112 mg
Sodium	1,359.5 mg
Potassium	195.5 mg
Total Carbohydrates	7 g
Dietary Fiber	0 g
Sugars	2 g
Protein	40.5 g

Easy Chicken Cacciatore

Serves 6

INGREDIENTS:

½ cup fat-free Italian dressing

3 pounds chicken thighs and drumsticks

1 cup sliced mushrooms

1 bag frozen onions and peppers

1 can diced tomatoes, with garlic

DIRECTIONS:

1. Heat a skillet over medium heat and add the Italian dressing. Add the chicken and cook until browned on all sides. Add the mushrooms, frozen vegetables, and tomatoes.

2. Turn heat down to low and cover. Simmer for 30 minutes, until chicken is cooked through.

NUTRITION FACTS

6 Servings

Amount Per Serving	
Calories	93
Total Fat	2 g
Saturated Fat	0.5 g
Polyunsaturated Fat	0.5 g
Monounsaturated Fat	0.5 g
Cholesterol	29.5 mg
Sodium	206 mg
Potassium	259.5 mg
Total Carbohydrates	7.5 g
Dietary Fiber	1 g
Sugars	2.5 g
Protein	11.5 g

Lemon Chicken and Broccoli

Serves 4

INGREDIENTS:

½ cup sugar-free Italian dressing

Zest and juice of 1 lemon

4 boneless, skinless chicken breasts,
   cut into strips

1 bag frozen broccoli

DIRECTIONS:

1. Combine the dressing, zest, and lemon juice. Heat a large skillet over medium heat and add half the dressing mixture, followed by the chicken strips. Cook until browned on both sides. Add broccoli.

2. Stir in remaining dressing, cover and cook for 5–7 minutes or until chicken is cooked through and broccoli is tender.

NUTRITION FACTS

4 Servings

Amount Per Serving	
Calories	203.5
Total Fat	8.5 g
Saturated Fat	2 g
Polyunsaturated Fat	0 g
Monounsaturated Fat	0 g
Cholesterol	70 mg
Sodium	582 mg
Potassium	192 mg
Total Carbohydrates	7 g
Dietary Fiber	2 g
Sugars	1.5 g
Protein	24 g

Best Roasted Chicken

Serves 4–6

INGREDIENTS

1 ¾ pound whole chicken

1 8-ounce bottle sugar-free Italian dressing

1 pound baby carrots

4 stalks celery, cut into chunks

DIRECTIONS:

1. Preheat oven to 350 degrees F.
2. Carefully separate the skin from the meat of the chicken. Brush the bottom with a quarter of the dressing. Tuck the wings under the breast and put the chicken on a roasting pan, breast side up.
3. Brush ½ cup of dressing under the skin and all around the outside of the chicken.
4. Add the carrots and celery to the roasting pan and drizzle remaining dressing over the vegetables.
5. Roast for 2 hours, or until chicken reaches 165 degrees. Allow to rest for 10 minutes before serving.

NUTRITION FACTS

4 Servings

Amount Per Serving	
Calories	229
Total Fat	13.5 g
Saturated Fat	2.5 g
Polyunsaturated Fat	0.5 g
Monounsaturated Fat	0.5 g
Cholesterol	25.5 mg
Sodium	591 mg
Potassium	627 mg
Total Carbohydrates	15 g
Dietary Fiber	4.5 g
Sugars	5 g
Protein	11 g

Greek Chicken

Serves 4–6

INGREDIENTS:

1 ¾ pound whole chicken

1 lemon

½ cup sugar-free Greek dressing

DIRECTIONS:

1. Preheat the oven to 350 degrees F.
2. Cut the lemon in half and squeeze the juice into a small bowl. Put the juiced pieces inside the chicken cavity.
3. Add the juice to the dressing and brush over the chicken.
4. Bake for 2 hours, or until chicken reaches 165 degrees. Allow to rest for 10 minutes before serving.

NUTRITION FACTS

4 Servings

Amount Per Serving	
Calories	115
Total Fat	7.5 g
Saturated Fat	1.5 g
Polyunsaturated Fat	0.5 g
Monounsaturated Fat	0.5 g
Cholesterol	25.5 mg
Sodium	237.5 mg
Potassium	95 mg
Total Carbohydrates	2 g
Dietary Fiber	0 g
Sugars	0.5 g
Protein	9.5 g

Ground Turkey Oven Loaf

Serves 12

INGREDIENTS:

1 cup fat-free shredded cheddar cheese

1 cup oyster crackers, crushed

½ cup chopped onion

1 cup fat-free milk

2 tablespoons sugar-free barbecue sauce

Dash of salt and pepper

¼ cup brown sugar

2 pounds lean ground turkey

DIRECTIONS:

1. Preheat oven to 350 degrees F. In a large bowl, mix together all ingredients except for ground turkey.

2. Add in ground turkey and mix well with hands.

3. Grease a 9 x 13 inch casserole dish and add beef mixture. Form into two side-by-side loaves.

4. Bake for 45 minutes.

NUTRITION FACTS

12 Servings

Amount Per Serving	
Calories	177.5
Total Fat	7.5 g
Saturated Fat	3 g
Polyunsaturated Fat	0 g
Monounsaturated Fat	0 g
Cholesterol	60.5 mg
Sodium	186.5 mg
Potassium	58 mg
Total Carbohydrates	11 g
Dietary Fiber	0 g
Sugars	7 g
Protein	18 g

Slow Cooked Turkey and Sweet Potatoes

Serves 12

INGREDIENTS:

6 pounds whole, fresh turkey breast, skin removed

2 teaspoons olive oil

Dash of salt and pepper

1 teaspoon Italian seasoning

2 onions, quartered

4 large sweet potatoes, quartered

½ cup water

DIRECTIONS:

1. Rinse turkey and pat dry with paper towels. Rub with oil and sprinkle with seasonings. Place in slow cooker.

2. Arrange onions and potatoes around turkey in slow cooker. Add water.

3. Cover and cook on low for 9–10 hours.

NUTRITION FACTS

12 Servings

Amount Per Serving	
Calories	112.5
Total Fat	2 g
Saturated Fat	0.5 g
Polyunsaturated Fat	0 g
Monounsaturated Fat	0.5 g
Cholesterol	24.5 mg
Sodium	228.5 mg
Potassium	117mg
Total Carbohydrates	12.5 g
Dietary Fiber	1.5 g
Sugars	0 g
Protein	10.5 g

Slow Cooker Thanksgiving Meal

Serves 6–8

INGREDIENTS:

1 box low-sodium stuffing mix

½ cup hot water

2 tablespoons butter, softened

1 cup chopped celery

½ cup dried cranberries

3-pound boneless turkey breast

1 teaspoon olive oil

Dash of salt and pepper

DIRECTIONS:

1. Add first 5 ingredients to slow cooker and mix well. Rub turkey breast with oil, and season with salt and pepper. Add to slow cooker.

2. Cook on Low 5–6 hours. Remove turkey and slice. Stir stuffing mixture before serving with turkey.

NUTRITION FACTS

8 Servings

Amount Per Serving	
Calories	378
Total Fat	10 g
Saturated Fat	2 g
Polyunsaturated Fat	0 g
Monounsaturated Fat	0.5 g
Cholesterol	117.5 mg
Sodium	1,222 mg
Potassium	46 mg
Total Carbohydrates	25.5 g
Dietary Fiber	1 g
Sugars	6.5 g
Protein	46.5 g

Italian 3-Ingredient Chicken

Serves 4

INGREDIENTS:

4 boneless, skinless chicken breasts
½ cup sugar-free Italian dressing
¾ cup Italian bread crumbs

DIRECTIONS:

1. Preheat oven to 350 degrees F. Lightly coat a 13 x 9 inch baking dish in olive oil cooking spray.
2. Arrange chicken breasts in baking dish. Pour dressing over chicken. Sprinkle bread crumbs on top.
3. Bake 25–35 minutes or until chicken is cooked through.

NUTRITION FACTS

4 Servings

Amount Per Serving	
Calories	266
Total Fat	9.5 g
Saturated Fat	2.5 g
Polyunsaturated Fat	0.5 g
Monounsaturated Fat	0.5 g
Cholesterol	70 mg
Sodium	966 mg
Potassium	52 mg
Total Carbohydrates	17.5 g
Dietary Fiber	1 g
Sugars	1.5 g
Protein	5 g

Crock pot Tropical Chicken

Serves: 8

INGREDIENTS:

- 5–6 boneless chicken breasts
- ¼ cup corn starch
- ¼ cup brown sugar
- ½ cup low-sodium soy sauce
- ¼ cup lemon juice
- 1 teaspoon ground ginger
- 1 16-ounce can of pineapple slices, drained and rinsed

DIRECTIONS:

1. Place chicken breasts in crock pot.
2. In a mixing bowl, whisk together corn starch, brown sugar, soy sauce, lemon juice, and ginger. Pour over chicken. Lay pineapples on top.
3. Cover and cook on Low for 4–5 hours.

NUTRITION FACTS

8 Servings

Amount Per Serving	
Calories	171.5
Total Fat	2 g
Saturated Fat	1 g
Polyunsaturated Fat	0 g
Monounsaturated Fat	0g
Cholesterol	52.5 mg
Sodium	840.5 mg
Potassium	101 mg
Total Carbohydrates	22 g
Dietary Fiber	0.5 g
Sugars	15 g
Protein	18 g

Juicy Tomato Chicken

Serves 6

INGREDIENTS:

2 tablespoons vegetable oil

6 boneless, skinless chicken breasts

2 15-ounce cans diced tomatoes

1 tablespoon Italian seasoning

1 cup low-sodium chicken stock

2 cups brown rice, cooked

DIRECTIONS:

1. Heat oil in a large skillet over medium heat. Add the chicken and brown on both sides. Add the tomatoes, Italian seasoning, and chicken stock.

2. Simmer over low heat for 20–25 minutes, until chicken is cooked through.

3. Shred the chicken and serve over brown rice.

NUTRITION FACTS

6 Servings

Amount Per Serving	
Calories	245.6
Total Fat	7.9 g
Saturated Fat	4.5 g
Polyunsaturated Fat	0.0 g
Monounsaturated Fat	0.0 g
Cholesterol	70.0 mg
Sodium	533.4 mg
Potassium	229.1 mg
Total Carbohydrates	18.6 g
Dietary Fiber	1.7 g
Sugars	1.6 g
Protein	24.4 g

Curried Chicken and Chickpeas

Serves 6

INGREDIENTS:

1 tablespoon olive oil

1 cup onion, chopped

6 chicken breasts, cubed

2 tablespoons curry powder

1 cup low-sodium chicken stock

2 cans chickpeas, drained and rinsed

DIRECTIONS:

1. Heat a large skillet over medium heat and add the oil, followed by the onions. Cook until onion is soft, then add the chicken.

2. Cook until chicken is browned on all sides and add curry powder, stock, and chickpeas. Simmer for 10 minutes.

NUTRITION FACTS

6 Servings

Amount Per Serving	
Calories	269
Total Fat	6 g
Saturated Fat	1.5 g
Polyunsaturated Fat	0.5 g
Monounsaturated Fat	2 g
Cholesterol	70 mg
Sodium	733.5 mg
Potassium	133 mg
Total Carbohydrates	22.5 g
Dietary Fiber	7 g
Sugars	1 g
Protein	29 g

Ground Turkey Tacos

Serves 4

INGREDIENTS:

- 1 pound ground turkey
- 1 teaspoon taco seasoning
- 8 corn taco shells
- ½ cup reduced-fat cheddar cheese
- 1 can diced tomatoes, drained and rinsed
- 8 large Iceberg lettuce leaves
- 1 cup nonfat sour cream

DIRECTIONS:

1. Brown the turkey in a large skillet over medium heat. Add taco seasoning and stir.
2. When turkey meat is fully cooked, scoop into taco shells and top with remaining ingredients as desired.

NUTRITION FACTS

4 Servings

Amount Per Serving	
Calories	353
Total Fat	16 g
Saturated Fat	6 g
Polyunsaturated Fat	0 g
Monounsaturated Fat	0 g
Cholesterol	96 mg
Sodium	348 mg
Potassium	229.5 mg
Total Carbohydrates	21 g
Dietary Fiber	1 g
Sugars	6 g
Protein	29 g

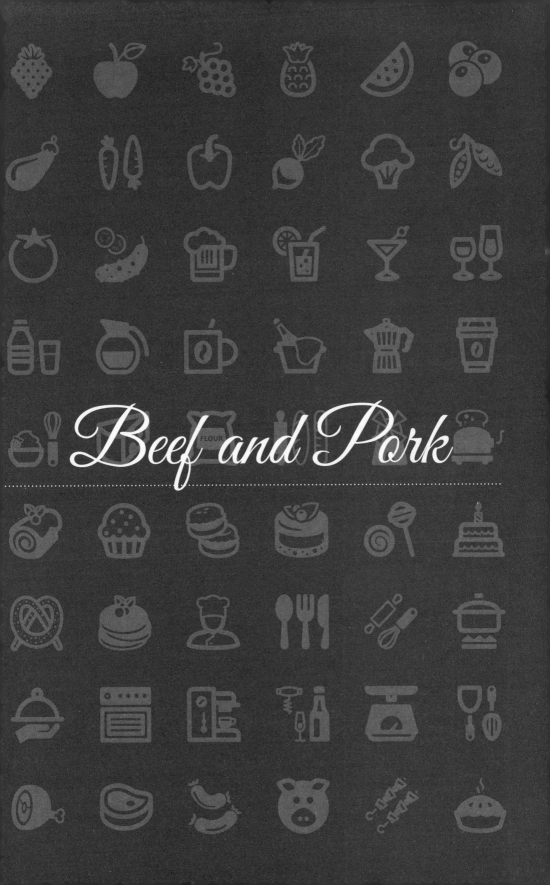

Beef and Pork

Apple Pork Chop Skillet

Serves 4

INGREDIENTS:

1 tablespoon olive oil

4 boneless pork chops

½ cup sugar-free barbecue sauce

2 apples, cored, peeled, and sliced

DIRECTIONS:

1. Preheat oven to 350 degrees F.
2. Heat a large oven-proof skillet over medium-high heat. Add the oil and pork chops. Cook until chops are browned on both sides. Add the barbecue sauce and arrange the apples around the pork.
3. Bake for 10–15 minutes, until apples are done and pork is tender.

NUTRITION FACTS

4 Servings

Amount Per Serving	
Calories	294
Total Fat	14.5 g
Saturated Fat	4.5 g
Polyunsaturated Fat	1.5 g
Monounsaturated Fat	7.5 g
Cholesterol	59 mg
Sodium	45 mg
Potassium	499.5 mg
Total Carbohydrates	16.5 g
Dietary Fiber	2 g
Sugars	9.5 g
Protein	21 g

Mushroom Pork Chops

Serves 4

INGREDIENTS:

4 regular cut bone-in pork chops

Nonstick cooking spray

1 can low-sodium cream of mushroom soup

1 cup uncooked brown rice

1 16-ounce bag frozen peas

2 ⅓ tablespoons dried onion flakes

1 teaspoon onion powder

¼ teaspoon celery seed

DIRECTIONS:

1. Preheat oven to 375 degrees F.
2. Spray a 9 x 13 inch pan with nonstick spray.
3. Combine mushroom soup, rice, and 2 cups hot water in the pan and stir until well mixed.
4. Stir in peas.
5. Arrange pork chops on top, pressing down into rice mixture.
6. Combine dry seasonings in a small bowl. Sprinkle over pork chops.
7. Bake 1 hour or until the pork chops are cooked through and the rice absorbs all liquid.

NUTRITION FACTS

4 Servings

Amount Per Serving	
Calories	601.5
Total Fat	31 g
Saturated Fat	10.5 g
Polyunsaturated Fat	4 g
Monounsaturated Fat	12.5 g
Cholesterol	84 mg
Sodium	610.5 mg
Potassium	953 mg
Total Carbohydrates	55.5 g
Dietary Fiber	6 g
Sugars	6 g
Protein	26 g

Beef and Broccoli Stir Fry

Serves 6

INGREDIENTS:

- 1 tablespoon olive oil or vegetable oil
- 1 pound sirloin steak, sliced
- 1 bag frozen broccoli florets
- ½ cup sugar-free Asian sesame salad dressing

DIRECTIONS:

1. Heat a large skillet over medium-high heat. Add the oil and steak and cook for 1 minute.

2. Add the broccoli and the salad dressing and continue cooking until broccoli is tender.

NUTRITION FACTS

6 Servings

Amount Per Serving	
Calories	240.5
Total Fat	18.5 g
Saturated Fat	5 g
Polyunsaturated Fat	0.5 g
Monounsaturated Fat	1.5 g
Cholesterol	50.5 mg
Sodium	201.5 mg
Potassium	118.5 mg
Total Carbohydrates	3 g
Dietary Fiber	1.5 g
Sugars	0.5 g
Protein	16.5 g

Salsa Beef Skillet

Serves 6

INGREDIENTS:

1 pound ground beef

1 16-ounce jar corn and black bean salsa

1 cup uncooked brown rice

1 cup shredded low-fat cheddar cheese

DIRECTIONS:

1. Heat a large skillet over medium heat. Add the beef and cook until it is no longer pink in the middle. Add the salsa, rice, and 1 cup water. Cover and cook for 20 minutes, until rice is tender.

2. Uncover, turn off heat, and add cheese. Serve when cheese is melted.

NUTRITION FACTS

6 Servings

Amount Per Serving	
Calories	323
Total Fat	20 g
Saturated Fat	8.5 g
Polyunsaturated Fat	0.5 g
Monounsaturated Fat	7 g
Cholesterol	70 mg
Sodium	435.5 mg
Potassium	210.5 mg
Total Carbohydrates	15.5 g
Dietary Fiber	0.5 g
Sugars	1.5 g
Protein	20.5 g

Slow Cooker Pork Chops

Serves 4

INGREDIENTS:

4 small onions, peeled and sliced

4 pork chops

½ teaspoon dried parsley

¼ teaspoon ground pepper

1 cup reduced-sodium beef broth

¼ cup prepared mustard

DIRECTIONS:

1. Line slow cooker with onions.

2. Sear pork shops in a skillet over medium-high heat. Place the pork chops on top of onions in the slow cooker. Sprinkle with parsley and pepper.

3. Whisk together mustard and beef broth. Pour into the slow cooker.

4. Cook on High for 3–4 hours or on low for 6–7 hours.

NUTRITION FACTS

4 Servings

Amount Per Serving	
Calories	140.5
Total Fat	4.5 g
Saturated Fat	1.5 g
Polyunsaturated Fat	0 g
Monounsaturated Fat	0.5 g
Cholesterol	45 mg
Sodium	1,257 mg
Potassium	133.5 mg
Total Carbohydrates	7.5 g
Dietary Fiber	2 g
Sugars	0 g
Protein	17g

Muffin Pan Cottage Pies

Serves 6

INGREDIENTS:

1 pound ground beef

1 box low-sodium stuffing mix

1 cup water

1 egg

1 bag frozen cauliflower, steamed and mashed

DIRECTIONS:

1. Preheat oven to 350 degrees F. Spray muffin pan with olive oil cooking spray.

2. In a large bowl, combine the ground beef, stuffing mix, water, and egg. Using your hands, mix it well.

3. Divide the meat mixture into muffin tins. Bake for 25–30 minutes until tops are browned.

4. Scoop a dollop of mashed cauliflower onto baked meatloaf muffins.

NUTRITION FACTS

6 Servings

Amount Per Serving	
Calories	333
Total Fat	17.5 g
Saturated Fat	6.5 g
Polyunsaturated Fat	1 g
Monounsaturated Fat	7 g
Cholesterol	87.5 mg
Sodium	325 mg
Potassium	292 mg
Total Carbohydrates	24.5 g
Dietary Fiber	1.5 g
Sugars	2.5 g
Protein	18.5 g

Brown Sugar Baked Pork Chops

Serves 6

INGREDIENTS:

2 tablespoons olive oil

6 boneless pork chops, fat trimmed (browned)

1 onion, sliced

1 green pepper, sliced

1 cup mushrooms, sliced

¼ cup brown sugar substitute

¼ cup ketchup

¼ cup lemon juice

DIRECTIONS:

1. Preheat oven to 350 degrees F. Grease a 9 x 13 inch casserole dish.
2. Place pork chops in casserole dish. Top with slices of onion, pepper, and mushrooms.
3. Whisk together brown sugar, ketchup, and lemon juice and pour over chops.
4. Cover with foil and bake 30 minutes. Remove cover and bake additional 30 minutes.

NUTRITION FACTS

6 Servings

Amount Per Serving	
Calories	210
Total Fat	9.5 g
Saturated Fat	2.5 g
Polyunsaturated Fat	0.5 g
Monounsaturated Fat	3.5 g
Cholesterol	55 mg
Sodium	708 mg
Potassium	78 mg
Total Carbohydrates	7.5 g
Dietary Fiber	1 g
Sugars	1 g
Protein	22 g

Pork and Cabbage Stir Fry

Serves 4

INGREDIENTS:

2 tablespoons oil

1 pound boneless pork chops, sliced into strips

2 cups shredded cabbage

1 tablespoon cornstarch

½ teaspoon ground ginger

¼ teaspoon garlic powder

½ cup water

1 tablespoon low-sodium soy sauce

DIRECTIONS:

1. Stir fry pork and oil in a skillet over medium-high heat.
2. Dump cabbage into skillet.
3. Mix together remaining ingredients and add to skillet. Cook until sauce thickens and pork is cooked through.

NUTRITION FACTS

4 Servings

Amount Per Serving	
Calories	215.5
Total Fat	12 g
Saturated Fat	2.5 g
Polyunsaturated Fat	2 g
Monounsaturated Fat	4 g
Cholesterol	55 mg
Sodium	752 mg
Potassium	109.5 mg
Total Carbohydrates	2.5 g
Dietary Fiber	1 g
Sugars	0g
Protein	22 g

Pork Loaf

Serves 9

INGREDIENTS:

1 pound extra-lean, low-sodium ground ham

1 pound ground pork tenderloin

1 egg

¼ cup chopped onion

½ cup Saltine crackers, crushed

½ cup fat-free milk

DIRECTIONS:

1. Preheat oven to 350 degrees F. Combine all ingredients in a large bowl.
2. Add to a greased loaf pan and bake for 1 ¼ hours or until well browned.

NUTRITION FACTS

9 Servings

Amount Per Serving	
Calories	234
Total Fat	13 g
Saturated Fat	4.5 g
Polyunsaturated Fat	1 g
Monounsaturated Fat	5 g
Cholesterol	99.5 mg
Sodium	554.5 mg
Potassium	224 mg
Total Carbohydrates	4 g
Dietary Fiber	0 g
Sugars	0.5 g
Protein	24.5 g

Mushroom Soup Pork Chops

Serves 4

INGREDIENTS:

1 tablespoon olive oil

4 pork chops, bone in, fat trimmed (browned)

1 (10.75-ounce) can low-sodium cream of
   mushroom soup

¾ cup water

½ teaspoon thyme

¼ teaspoon rosemary

DIRECTIONS:

1. Preheat oven to 350 degrees F. Arrange
   pork chops in a 9 x 13 inch casserole dish.

2. Mix together remaining ingredients in
   a small bowl and pour over chops.

3. Cover with foil and bake for 50 minutes.
   Uncover and bake 10 more minutes.

NUTRITION FACTS

4 Servings

Amount Per Serving	
Calories	291.5
Total Fat	18.5 g
Saturated Fat	5.5 g
Polyunsaturated Fat	2 g
Monounsaturated Fat	8g
Cholesterol	67 mg
Sodium	539.5 mg
Potassium	341 mg
Total Carbohydrates	5 g
Dietary Fiber	0 g
Sugars	0 g
Protein	25 g

Cheesy Ham, Broccoli and Rice

Serves 4

INGREDIENTS:

- 1 10.75 ounce can low-sodium condensed cream of mushroom soup
- 1 cup low-fat milk
- 1 cup ham, diced
- 2 cups broccoli florets
- 1 cup brown rice, uncooked
- 1 cup shredded reduced-fat cheddar cheese

DIRECTIONS:

1. Whisk together soup and milk in slow cooker until smooth. Add remaining ingredients.
2. Cover and cook on Low for 2 hours. Stir. Cook on Low for 2 more hours.

NUTRITION FACTS

4 Servings

Amount Per Serving	
Calories	386.5
Total Fat	13 g
Saturated Fat	6 g
Polyunsaturated Fat	1 g
Monounsaturated Fat	1.5 g
Cholesterol	48.5 mg
Sodium	1,106.5 mg
Potassium	778.5 mg
Total Carbohydrates	48 g
Dietary Fiber	4 g
Sugars	4.5 g
Protein	21.5 g

Asian Pot Roast

Serves 6

INGREDIENTS:

1 tablespoon olive oil

1 4–5 pound roast

1 onion, sliced

¼ cup low-sodium soy sauce

¼ cup fat-free Asian sesame salad dressing

2 ½ cups low-sodium beef stock

2 cups brown rice, cooked

DIRECTIONS:

1. Heat a large Dutch oven over medium heat. Add the olive oil followed by the roast. Sear the roast until browned on all sides.

2. Add the onions, soy sauce, salad dressing, and stock.

3. Bring to a simmer, cover, and cook over low heat for 3–4 hours, until the pot roast falls apart easily with a fork.

4. Serve with brown rice.

NUTRITION FACTS

6 Servings

Amount Per Serving	
Calories	572
Total Fat	33g
Saturated Fat	2.5 g
Polyunsaturated Fat	0.5 g
Monounsaturated Fat	4 g
Cholesterol	90.5 mg
Sodium	799 mg
Potassium	643 mg
Total Carbohydrates	19.5 g
Dietary Fiber	1.5 g
Sugars	1.5 g
Protein	46.5 g

Slow Cooker Baked Beans

Serves 12

INGREDIENTS:

- 3 28-ounce cans no salt added baked beans, drained
- 1 onion, chopped
- ²/₃ cup sugar-free barbecue sauce
- 1 cup extra-lean, reduced-sodium ham
- 1 tablespoon dry mustard
- ¼ cup sweet pickle relish

DIRECTIONS:

1. Add all ingredients to a slow cooker and cook on high for 3 hours or on low for 6 hours.

NUTRITION FACTS

12 Servings

Amount Per Serving	
Calories	250
Total Fat	0.5 g
Saturated Fat	0 g
Polyunsaturated Fat	0 g
Monounsaturated Fat	0.5 g
Cholesterol	5.5 mg
Sodium	1,106 mg
Potassium	54 mg
Total Carbohydrates	52 g
Dietary Fiber	8.5 g
Sugars	20.5 g
Protein	12.5 g

Sausage Scrambler

Serves 4

INGREDIENTS:

8 large eggs

¼ cup milk

1 tablespoon olive oil

¼ cup cooked and crumbled breakfast sausage

½ cup reduced-fat cheddar cheese

DIRECTIONS:

1. Beat the eggs and milk together. Heat a large skillet over medium heat and add oil to skillet.

2. Pour the egg mixture in the skillet and stir in sausage. Stir the eggs intermittently until cooked through.

3. Sprinkle cheese over cooked eggs and serve.

NUTRITION FACTS

4 Servings

Amount Per Serving	
Calories	280.5
Total Fat	19 g
Saturated Fat	7.5 g
Polyunsaturated Fat	2.5 g
Monounsaturated Fat	6 g
Cholesterol	393 mg
Sodium	422 mg
Potassium	162 mg
Total Carbohydrates	1.5 g
Dietary Fiber	0 g
Sugars	1 g
Protein	19 g

Soups and Stews

White Bean Chili

Serves 2

INGREDIENTS:

1 teaspoon canola oil

½ cup chopped onion

1 clove garlic, minced

½ teaspoon ground cumin

¼ teaspoon dried oregano

Pinch cayenne pepper

Pinch ground cloves

2 cups low-sodium canned chicken broth

1 15-ounce can white beans, rinsed

1 tablespoon dried parsley

Salt and pepper, to taste

DIRECTIONS:

1. Heat oil, onion, and garlic on low in a large nonstick saucepan. Allow onions to soften.
2. Stir in seasonings.
3. Add 2 cups of the chicken broth slowly while stirring.
4. Add in beans and parsley. Cover and simmer for 15 minutes, stirring occasionally. If chili is too thick, add additional broth until it's the desired consistency.
5. Add salt and pepper to taste.

NUTRITION FACTS

2 Servings

Amount Per Serving	
Calories	330.5
Total Fat	3.5 g
Saturated Fat	0.5 g
Polyunsaturated Fat	1 g
Monounsaturated Fat	1.5 g
Cholesterol	0 mg
Sodium	627 mg
Potassium	1,528.5 mg
Total Carbohydrates	57 g
Dietary Fiber	12.5 g
Sugars	0 g
Protein	20.5 g

Chicken and Bean Soup

Serves 4

INGREDIENTS:

- 2 cups chicken breasts, chopped
- 3 cups low-sodium chicken stock
- 2 cans white beans, drained and rinsed
- 1 tablespoon Italian dressing seasoning
- 1 10-ounce package frozen spinach, chopped

DIRECTIONS:

1. Combine all ingredients in a large saucepan with 2 cups water. Bring to a boil and reduce to a simmer.
2. Simmer for 10–15 minutes, until chicken is cooked through and soup is hot.

NUTRITION FACTS

4 Servings

Amount Per Serving	
Calories	244.5
Total Fat	3 g
Saturated Fat	1 g
Polyunsaturated Fat	0.5 g
Monounsaturated Fat	1 g
Cholesterol	70 mg
Sodium	784 mg
Potassium	861 mg
Total Carbohydrates	21 g
Dietary Fiber	7 g
Sugars	1.5 g
Protein	35.5 g

Chicken and Black Bean Soup

Serves 6

INGREDIENTS:

2 cups chopped or shredded cooked chicken

3 cups water

1 14-ounce can reduced-sodium chicken broth

1 14-ounce can diced tomatoes, undrained

1 4 ½ ounce cans green chilies

½ cup frozen corn or canned corn, drained

1 16-ounce can black beans, drained and rinsed

1 teaspoon cumin

1 tablespoon chili powder

DIRECTIONS:

1. Combine all of the ingredients in a large pot.
2. Bring to a boil.
3. Reduce to a simmer. Simmer for 10 minutes, or until heated through.

NUTRITION FACTS

6 Servings

Amount Per Serving	
Calories	172
Total Fat	2.5 g
Saturated Fat	0.5 g
Polyunsaturated Fat	0.5 g
Monounsaturated Fat	1 g
Cholesterol	35 mg
Sodium	471.5 mg
Potassium	678.5 mg
Total Carbohydrates	21.5 g
Dietary Fiber	5.5 g
Sugars	2 g
Protein	19 g

Chicken Sausage Corn Chowder

Serves 4

INGREDIENTS:

1 tablespoon olive oil or vegetable oil

3 chicken sausage links, sliced

1 onion, chopped

1 6.5 ounce can baby clams

1 can no-salt-added crushed tomatoes

DIRECTIONS:

1. In a medium saucepan, heat the oil. Add the sausage and onion and cook until sausage is browned.

2. Add the clams and tomatoes. Stir and cook until heated through.

NUTRITION FACTS

4 Servings

Amount Per Serving	
Calories	201.5
Total Fat	10 g
Saturated Fat	2.5 g
Polyunsaturated Fat	0.5 g
Monounsaturated Fat	2.5 g
Cholesterol	62.5 mg
Sodium	394 mg
Potassium	352 mg
Total Carbohydrates	6 g
Dietary Fiber	1 g
Sugars	0 g
Protein	20 g

Italian Chicken Vegetable Soup

Serves 4

INGREDIENTS:

1 teaspoon olive oil or vegetable oil

2 cups chopped chicken breast

1 15-ounce can green beans, drained and rinsed

1 15-ounce can low-sodium chicken broth

1 15-ounce can white beans of your choice, drained and rinsed

1 15-ounce can diced tomatoes, drained and rinsed

1 10-ounce package frozen spinach, broken up

¼ cup dried parsley

½ teaspoon dried basil

½ teaspoon ground black pepper

DIRECTIONS:

1. Heat a teaspoon of oil in a large pot. Add the chicken and brown.

2. Add remaining ingredients to pot and bring to a boil. Reduce heat to simmer. Simmer until chicken is cooked through and soup is hot.

NUTRITION FACTS

4 Servings

Amount Per Serving	
Calories	228
Total Fat	4 g
Saturated Fat	1 g
Polyunsaturated Fat	1 g
Monounsaturated Fat	2 g
Cholesterol	52.5 mg
Sodium	924 mg
Potassium	550.5 mg
Total Carbohydrate	12.5 g
Dietary Fiber	8 g
Sugars	3.5 g
Protein	27.5 g

Chicken Tortilla Soup

Serves 4

INGREDIENTS:

1 15-ounce can black beans, drained and rinsed

1 15-ounce can low sodium chicken broth

1 15-ounce can diced tomatoes, drained and rinsed

1 15-ounce can corn, drained and rinsed

2 cups shredded or chopped cooked chicken

1 cup unsalted tortilla chips, crushed

DIRECTIONS:

1. Dump beans, broth, tomatoes, and corn in a soup pot. Add the chicken.

2. Add the chicken, and bring to a boil. Reduce heat to a simmer.

3. Serve hot, topped with crushed tortilla chips.

NUTRITION FACTS

4 Servings

Amount Per Serving	
Calories	418
Total Fat	10 g
Saturated Fat	1.5 g
Polyunsaturated Fat	1 g
Monounsaturated Fat	1.5 g
Cholesterol	52.5 mg
Sodium	958 mg
Potassium	773.5 mg
Total Carbohydrates	53.5 g
Dietary Fiber	12 g
Sugars	1.5 g
Protein	32.5 g

Pumpkin Pie Soup

Serves 4

INGREDIENTS:

- ¾ cup water, divided
- 1 15-ounce can pumpkin puree
- 2 cups unsalted vegetable broth
- ½ teaspoon ground cinnamon
- ¼ teaspoon ground nutmeg
- 1 cup whole milk

DIRECTIONS:

1. In a large saucepan over medium-high heat, combine the first 5 ingredients. Bring to a boil and then reduce heat to a simmer.
2. Once simmering, stir in the milk. Cook until hot, but don't boil. Serve immediately.

NUTRITION FACTS

4 Servings

Amount Per Serving	
Calories	86.5
Total Fat	2.5 g
Saturated Fat	1.5 g
Polyunsaturated Fat	0 g
Monounsaturated Fat	0 g
Cholesterol	9 mg
Sodium	106 mg
Potassium	352.5 mg
Total Carbohydrates	14.5 g
Dietary Fiber	4 g
Sugars	8 g
Protein	3.5 g

Simple Minestrone

Serves 4

INGREDIENTS:

1 15-ounce cans low sodium chicken broth

1 15-ounce can chickpeas, drained and rinsed

1 15-ounce can no-salt-added diced tomatoes

1 bag Italian style frozen vegetables

½ cup whole grain pasta, like elbows

¼ cup sugar-free Italian dressing

DIRECTIONS:

1. Combine all ingredients in a large saucepan. Bring to a boil.

2. Reduce heat and simmer for 8–10 minutes, until pasta is tender. Serve hot.

NUTRITION FACTS

4 Servings

Amount Per Serving	
Calories	347.5
Total Fat	5.5 g
Saturated Fat	0.5 g
Polyunsaturated Fat	1 g
Monounsaturated Fat	0.5 g
Cholesterol	0 mg
Sodium	819 mg
Potassium	805.5 mg
Total Carbohydrates	63 g
Dietary Fiber	12.5 g
Sugars	1 g
Protein	14 g

Tortellini Soup

Serves 4

INGREDIENTS:

- 2 15-ounce cans low-sodium chicken broth
- 1 9-ounce package whole-wheat cheese tortellini
- 1 15-ounce can (no-sugar-added) Italian style stewed tomatoes
- 1 10-ounce package frozen spinach, chopped
- 2 garlic cloves, minced or ¼ teaspoon garlic powder

Salt and pepper, to taste

DIRECTIONS:

1. Bring chicken broth to a boil. Add the tortellini and cook for about 6 minutes.
2. In the same pot, add the rest of the ingredients. Stir and simmer for 10 minutes. Serve hot.

NUTRITION FACTS

4 Servings

Amount Per Serving	
Calories	180
Total Fat	6.5 g
Saturated Fat	3 g
Polyunsaturated Fat	0 g
Monounsaturated Fat	0 g
Cholesterol	24 mg
Sodium	976.5 mg
Potassium	794.5 mg
Total Carbohydrates	22 g
Dietary Fiber	4 g
Sugars	2 g
Protein	11 g

Mushroom Barley Slow Cooker Soup

Serves 8

INGREDIENTS:

4 15-ounce cans low-sodium beef broth

1 cup water

1 pound mushrooms, sliced

1 medium onion, diced

2 carrots, diced

½ teaspoon salt

½ teaspoon fresh ground pepper

½ teaspoon dried thyme

¼ teaspoon dried sage

1 cup barley

DIRECTIONS:

1. Add all ingredients to slow cooker and stir gently to combine.
2. Cover, and cook on Low for 6–7 hours.

NUTRITION FACTS

8 Servings

Amount Per Serving	
Calories	127
Total Fat	0.5 g
Saturated Fat	0 g
Polyunsaturated Fat	0.5 g
Monounsaturated Fat	0 g
Cholesterol	0 mg
Sodium	601 mg
Potassium	318.5 mg
Total Carbohydrates	25 g
Dietary Fiber	5.5 g
Sugars	2 g
Protein	7.5 g

Easy Game Day Chili

Serves 4

INGREDIENTS:

- 1 pound cooked lean ground beef
- 2 15-ounce cans pinto beans, drained and rinsed
- 1 15-ounce can diced tomatoes, drained and rinsed
- 1 onion, minced
- 2 tablespoons chili powder

DIRECTIONS:

1. Combine all ingredients in a large soup pot.
2. Bring to a boil. Reduce heat and simmer for 20–25 minutes until thickened.

NUTRITION FACTS

4 Servings

Amount Per Serving	
Calories	504.5
Total Fat	24.5 g
Saturated Fat	9.5 g
Polyunsaturated Fat	1.5 g
Monounsaturated Fat	10.5 g
Cholesterol	85 mg
Sodium	1,029 mg
Potassium	1,303.5 mg
Total Carbohydrates	47.5 g
Dietary Fiber	17 g
Sugars	0.5 g
Protein	34 g

Chicken Noodle Soup

Serves 6–8

INGREDIENTS:

1 tablespoon olive oil

2 cups chopped chicken

1 onion, chopped

2 ribs celery, chopped

2 carrots, chopped

2 15-ounce cans low-sodium chicken broth

4 cups water

2 cups low-sodium egg white noodles

1 teaspoon Italian seasoning

DIRECTIONS:

1. Heat the olive oil in a large soup pot. Add the chicken, onions, celery, and carrots.

2. Cook until tender, about 10 minutes.

3. Add broth, noodles, and seasoning.

4. Bring to a boil. Reduce heat and simmer for 20 minutes. Serve hot.

NUTRITION FACTS

6 Servings

Amount Per Serving	
Calories	167
Total Fat	5 g
Saturated Fat	1 g
Polyunsaturated Fat	1 g
Monounsaturated Fat	2.5 g
Cholesterol	47 mg
Sodium	466 mg
Potassium	529.5 mg
Total Carbohydrates	13.5 g
Dietary Fiber	1.5 g
Sugars	1 g
Protein	16.5 g

Homemade Vegetable Soup

Serves 4

INGREDIENTS:

- 1 15-ounce can low-sodium chicken or vegetable broth
- 2 cups water
- 1 medium sweet potato, peeled and diced
- 1 15-ounce can no-salt added diced tomatoes, drained and rinsed
- 1 15-ounce can green beans, drained and rinsed
- 1 15-ounce can white beans, drained and rinsed
- 2 ribs celery, chopped
- ¼ teaspoon fresh ground pepper

DIRECTIONS:

1. Combine all ingredients in a large soup pot.
2. Bring to a boil and then reduce to a simmer.
3. Simmer for 10–15 minutes. Serve hot.

NUTRITION FACTS

4 Servings

Amount Per Serving	
Calories	151.5
Total Fat	0 g
Saturated Fat	0 g
Polyunsaturated Fat	0 g
Monounsaturated Fat	0 g
Cholesterol	0 mg
Sodium	967.5 mg
Potassium	644 mg
Total Carbohydrates	31.5 g
Dietary Fiber	9 g
Sugars	2 g
Protein	8.5 g

Seafood Corn Chowder

Serves 4

INGREDIENTS:

- 3 cups low-sodium chicken broth
- 3 cups diced red potatoes
- 1 16-ounce package frozen corn, thawed
- 1 bunch chopped scallions
- ½ pound thawed shrimp, peeled, deveined, and cut in half
- ¼ cup heavy cream or sour cream
- 1 tablespoon fresh lemon juice

DIRECTIONS:

1. In a medium saucepan, boil broth and potatoes for 5 minutes. Add corn and scallion and allow to simmer for 8 minutes.
2. Stir in shrimp. Cook until bright pink. Stir in cream, lemon juice, and scallion greens. Season with salt and freshly ground black pepper.

NUTRITION FACTS

4 Servings

Amount Per Serving	
Calories	267.5
Total Fat	5 g
Saturated Fat	2 g
Polyunsaturated Fat	1 g
Monounsaturated Fat	1 g
Cholesterol	92.5 mg
Sodium	576 mg
Potassium	1,161.5 mg
Total Carbohydrates	40.5 g
Dietary Fiber	5.5 g
Sugars	5 g
Protein	19 g

Split Pea Soup

Serves 12–14

INGREDIENTS:

1 tablespoon vegetable oil

1 onion, chopped

2 stalks celery, chopped

1 cup sliced carrots

2 cloves garlic, minced

2 cups split peas

1 cup uncooked brown rice, rinsed

8 cups water

Salt and pepper to taste

DIRECTIONS:

1. Heat oil in a large soup pot and sauté onion, celery, carrots, and garlic until tender. Add split peas, rice, and water. Bring to a boil, reduce heat, and cover.

2. Simmer for 1–2 hours or until peas and rice are tender. Add salt and pepper and serve hot.

NUTRITION FACTS

12 Servings

Amount Per Serving	
Calories	94.5
Total Fat	1.5 g
Saturated Fat	1 g
Polyunsaturated Fat	0 g
Monounsaturated Fat	0 g
Cholesterol	0 mg
Sodium	14.5 mg
Potassium	213.5 mg
Total Carbohydrates	16.5 g
Dietary Fiber	4 g
Sugars	1.5 g
Protein	4 g

Easy Beef Stew

Serves 6

INGREDIENTS:

2 pounds beef for stewing, cubed

3 carrots, sliced

4 ribs celery, sliced

1 onion, chopped

1 10.75-ounce can no-salt-added tomato soup

1 ½ cups water

Dash salt and pepper

1 tablespoon balsamic vinegar

4 medium-sized potatoes, peeled and cubed

DIRECTIONS:

1. Add ingredients to a slow cooker and stir. Cook on low for 10–12 hours.

NUTRITION FACTS

6 Servings

Amount Per Serving	
Calories	598.5
Total Fat	30 g
Saturated Fat	2.5 g
Polyunsaturated Fat	0.5 g
Monounsaturated Fat	2 g
Cholesterol	93 mg
Sodium	233.5 mg
Potassium	1,361 mg
Total Carbohydrates	33 g
Dietary Fiber	6 g
Sugars	6 g
Protein	46.5 g

Coconut Chicken Soup

Serves 4

INGREDIENTS:

3 chicken breasts, cooked and cubed

3 cups low-sodium chicken stock

1 tablespoon curry powder

½ cup green onion, chopped

1 can light coconut milk

DIRECTIONS:

1. Add chicken stock and chicken to medium saucepan and bring to a boil.
2. Reduce to a simmer and add remaining ingredients. Stir and simmer until heated through.

NUTRITION FACTS

4 Servings

Amount Per Serving	
Calories	286.5
Total Fat	19.5 g
Saturated Fat	14.5 g
Polyunsaturated Fat	0 g
Monounsaturated Fat	0 g
Cholesterol	60 mg
Sodium	1,441.5 mg
Potassium	33.5 mg
Total Carbohydrates	7.5 g
Dietary Fiber	0 g
Sugars	2.5 g
Protein	19.5 g

Thai Chicken Soup

Serves 6

INGREDIENTS:

- 2 tablespoons olive oil
- 3 cups chicken breast
- 2 garlic cloves, minced
- 2 tablespoons white wine or rice wine vinegar
- ¼ cup low-sodium teriyaki sauce
- ½ cup water
- 2 cups low-sodium chicken stock
- ¼ cup reduced-sodium, no-added sugar, creamy peanut butter

DIRECTIONS:

1. Heat oil in a Dutch oven over medium heat. Brown the chicken in oil.
2. Add garlic, wine, and teriyaki sauce, and cook until chicken is no longer pink in the middle.
3. Add the water, chicken stock, and peanut butter, and stir until well combined.

NUTRITION FACTS

6 Servings

Amount Per Serving	
Calories	232.5
Total Fat	12.5 g
Saturated Fat	2 g
Polyunsaturated Fat	2.5 g
Monounsaturated Fat	7 g
Cholesterol	52.5 mg
Sodium	344.5 mg
Potassium	294.5 mg
Total Carbohydrates	4.5 g
Dietary Fiber	0.5 g
Sugars	1 g
Protein	22 g

Fish and Seafood

Shrimp Scampi

Serves 6

INGREDIENTS:

¼ cup low-sodium chicken broth

½ cup white wine

2 tablespoons olive oil

1 tablespoon butter

1 tablespoon minced garlic

2 tablespoons parsley, finely chopped

1 tablespoon lemon juice

Salt and pepper to taste

½ teaspoon red pepper flakes

1 pound raw shrimp, peeled and deveined

DIRECTIONS:

1. Add broth, wine, olive oil, butter, garlic, parsley, lemon juice, salt, pepper, and red pepper flakes to skillet over medium heat. Stir until fully combined.
2. Add shrimp. Cook until shrimp is opaque. Serve.

NUTRITION FACTS

6 Servings

Amount Per Serving	
Calories	147.5
Total Fat	7.5 g
Saturated Fat	2 g
Polyunsaturated Fat	1 g
Monounsaturated Fat	4 g
Cholesterol	152.5 mg
Sodium	210 mg
Potassium	179 mg
Total Carbohydrates	0.5 g
Dietary Fiber	0 g
Sugars	0 g
Protein	16 g

Cheesy Fish Casserole

Serves 4

INGREDIENTS:

- 1 ½ cups low-fat milk
- ¼ cup low-fat shredded cheddar cheese
- ¼ cup low-fat shredded Swiss cheese
- 1 tablespoon parmesan cheese
- 2 teaspoons Worcestershire sauce
- 1 pound fresh or frozen cod, cut into bite-size pieces

DIRECTIONS:

1. Preheat oven to 350 degrees F.
2. Heat milk in a saucepan, but do not boil.
3. Add all three cheeses and Worcestershire sauce to saucepan. Stir until melted.
4. Place fish in a 9x9 inch baking dish coated with olive oil.
5. Pour sauce over top and bake for 30 minutes, or until fish is opaque and flaky inside.

NUTRITION FACTS

4 Servings

Amount Per Serving	
Calories	277
Total Fat	11 g
Saturated Fat	6.5 g
Polyunsaturated Fat	0.5 g
Monounsaturated Fat	2 g
Cholesterol	99 mg
Sodium	422 mg
Potassium	435.5 mg
Total Carbohydrates	6.5 g
Dietary Fiber	0 g
Sugars	5 g
Protein	36 g

Tuna Onion Casserole

Serves 6

INGREDIENTS:

- 1 bag whole-wheat egg white egg noodles, cooked
- ½ cup chopped onion
- 2 6-ounce cans tuna in water, drained
- 2 10.5-ounce cans low-sodium cream of mushroom soup
- 1 bag frozen mixed peas and carrots (drained)
- ½ cup reduced-fat cheddar cheese
- ½ cup reduced-fat mozzarella cheese

DIRECTIONS:

1. Preheat oven to 350 degrees F. Combine ingredients (except cheese) in a large bowl and empty into a 13 x 9 inch baking dish coated in olive oil cooking spray.
2. Sprinkle cheese on top and bake 25 minutes, or until heated through.

NUTRITION FACTS

6 Servings

Amount Per Serving	
Calories	396.5
Total Fat	11.5 g
Saturated Fat	4 g
Polyunsaturated Fat	2.5 g
Monounsaturated Fat	1 g
Cholesterol	31 mg
Sodium	977.5 mg
Potassium	274.5 mg
Total Carbohydrates	54.5 g
Dietary Fiber	8 g
Sugars	0 g
Protein	27 g

Zesty Cod Bake

Serves 4

INGREDIENTS:

4 (6 ounce) fresh or frozen cod fillets

1 jar salsa

DIRECTIONS:

1. Preheat oven to 425 degrees F. Lightly coat a 13 x 9 inch baking dish in olive oil cooking spray.

2. Place cod fillets in baking dish and cover in salsa. Bake 15 minutes if fresh, 25 minutes if frozen. Fish should be opaque and flake easily with a fork.

NUTRITION FACTS

4 Servings

Amount Per Serving	
Calories	175
Total Fat	1 g
Saturated Fat	0 g
Polyunsaturated Fat	0 g
Monounsaturated Fat	0 g
Cholesterol	60 mg
Sodium	880 mg
Potassium	0 mg
Total Carbohydrates	8 g
Dietary Fiber	0 g
Sugars	4 g
Protein	30 g

Italian Cod Bake

Serves 4

INGREDIENTS:

4 (6 ounce) fresh or frozen cod fillets

½ cup sugar-free Italian dressing

¾ cup Italian breadcrumbs

DIRECTIONS:

1. Preheat oven to 425 degrees F. Lightly coat a 13 x 9 inch baking dish in olive oil cooking spray.
2. Arrange cod fillets in baking dish. Pour dressing over fish. Sprinkle breadcrumbs on top.
3. Bake 15 minutes if fresh, 25–30 minutes if frozen. Fish should be opaque and flake easily with a fork.

NUTRITION FACTS

4 Servings

Amount Per Serving	
Calories	281
Total Fat	8 g
Saturated Fat	1.5 g
Polyunsaturated Fat	0.5 g
Monounsaturated Fat	0.5 g
Cholesterol	60 mg
Sodium	736 mg
Potassium	52 mg
Total Carbohydrates	16.5 g
Dietary Fiber	1 g
Sugars	1.5 g
Protein	33 g

Cracker Crumb Baked Fish

Serves 4

INGREDIENTS:

- 4 (6-ounce) fresh or frozen cod or haddock fillets
- 1 cup light mayonnaise
- 1 sleeve whole-wheat Ritz crackers, crushed
- ½ teaspoon garlic powder

DIRECTIONS:

1. Preheat oven to 350 degrees F. Spread mayonnaise on both sides of fish fillets.
2. Roll fillets in cracker crumbs.
3. Place in 13 x 9 inch baking dish coated in olive oil cooking spray. Bake for 25–30 minutes, or until fish flakes easily with a fork.

NUTRITION FACTS

4 Servings

Amount Per Serving	
Calories	345
Total Fat	15.5 g
Saturated Fat	0.5 g
Polyunsaturated Fat	8 g
Monounsaturated Fat	2 g
Cholesterol	60 mg
Sodium	620 mg
Potassium	31 mg
Total Carbohydrates	19 g
Dietary Fiber	1 g
Sugars	6 g
Protein	31.5 g

Fish Tacos

Serves 4

INGREDIENTS:

- 1 14-ounce can salmon, drained
- 1 8-ounce can Rotel, drained and rinsed
- 1 tablespoon lime juice
- 8 6-inch corn tortillas, warmed
- 1 bag fresh coleslaw mix
- 1 medium avocado, sliced
- 1 cup fat-free sour cream

DIRECTIONS:

1. Mix together first 3 ingredients in a skillet over low heat.
2. Spoon into warm tortillas. Top with coleslaw, avocado, and sour cream.

NUTRITION FACTS

4 Servings

Amount Per Serving	
Calories	384
Total Fat	14 g
Saturated Fat	3 g
Polyunsaturated Fat	3.5 g
Monounsaturated Fat	6.5 g
Cholesterol	54.5 mg
Sodium	281.5 mg
Potassium	648.5 mg
Total Carbohydrates	38 g
Dietary Fiber	7.5 g
Sugars	7 g
Protein	26 g

Parmesan Crusted Cod Bake

Serves 4

INGREDIENTS:

1 cup light mayonnaise

½ cup grated reduced-fat parmesan cheese

2 tablespoons Worcestershire sauce

4 (6-ounce) cod or haddock fillets

DIRECTIONS:

1. Preheat oven to 350 degrees F. Lightly coat a 13 x 9 inch baking dish in olive oil cooking spray.

2. Mix together first 3 ingredients. Arrange cod fillets in baking dish.

3. Spread mayonnaise mixture over fish. Bake 25–30 minutes, uncovered. Fish should be opaque and flake easily with a fork.

NUTRITION FACTS

4 Servings

Amount Per Serving	
Calories	337
Total Fat	16.5 g
Saturated Fat	2.5 g
Polyunsaturated Fat	8 g
Monounsaturated Fat	3 g
Cholesterol	70 mg
Sodium	847.5 mg
Potassium	44.5 mg
Total Carbohydrates	9.5 g
Dietary Fiber	0 g
Sugars	5 g
Protein	35.5 g

Tuna Salad Stuffed Tomatoes

Serves 4

INGREDIENTS:

4 large tomatoes

1 14-ounce can tuna in water, drained

¾ cup light mayonnaise

1 teaspoon lemon juice

Dash of pepper

DIRECTIONS:

1. Preheat oven to 400 degrees F. Cut a thin slice off the top of each tomato. Hollow out the center by removing the pulp. Place tomatoes upside down on paper towels.

2. Combine remaining ingredients to make tuna salad.

3. Stuff a scoop of tuna salad into each tomato. Bake for 15–20 minutes.

NUTRITION FACTS

4 Servings

Amount Per Serving	
Calories	227
Total Fat	10.5 g
Saturated Fat	1 g
Polyunsaturated Fat	6.5 g
Monounsaturated Fat	1.5 g
Cholesterol	35 mg
Sodium	546.5 mg
Potassium	606 mg
Total Carbohydrates	14.5 g
Dietary Fiber	2 g
Sugars	3 g
Protein	21 g

Fast and Easy Fish Cakes

Serves 3–4

INGREDIENTS:

- 1 pound fresh or frozen firm, white fish like cod or haddock
- 1 cup water
- 1 egg, beaten
- 1 garlic clove, minced
- 2 tablespoons green onion, chopped
- 1 tablespoon lemon juice
- 8–10 crushed Ritz crackers
- 2 tablespoons olive oil
- 1 bag salad spring mix

DIRECTIONS:

1. Cook fish in a skillet in one cup of water for 10–15 minutes, breaking fish into smaller pieces; drain. Add remaining ingredients to skillet and mix together.
2. Shape mixture into patties and brown patties in skillet for 8 minutes on each side. Serve over salad greens.

NUTRITION FACTS

4 Servings

Amount Per Serving	
Calories	245.5
Total Fat	11 g
Saturated Fat	2 g
Polyunsaturated Fat	2 g
Monounsaturated Fat	6 g
Cholesterol	109 mg
Sodium	164 mg
Potassium	304.5 mg
Total Carbohydrates	7 g
Dietary Fiber	0.5 g
Sugars	1.5 g
Protein	28 g

Fast and Easy Shrimp Cakes

Serves 4

INGREDIENTS:

2 4-ounce cans tiny shrimp, drained and rinsed

1 egg, beaten

1 garlic clove, minced

1 tablespoon lemon juice

8–10 crushed Ritz crackers

2 tablespoons olive oil

1 bag salad spring mix

DIRECTIONS:

1. Add all ingredients (except salad mix) to a skillet and cook over medium-low heat. Stir until combined.
2. Shape mixture into patties and brown patties in skillet for 8 minutes on each side.
3. Serve over salad greens.

NUTRITION FACTS

4 Servings

Amount Per Serving	
Calories	186.5
Total Fat	10 g
Saturated Fat	2 g
Polyunsaturated Fat	2 g
Monounsaturated Fat	6 g
Cholesterol	106.5 mg
Sodium	275.5 mg
Potassium	28 mg
Total Carbohydrates	7 g
Dietary Fiber	0.5 g
Sugars	1.5 g
Protein	15.5 g

Fast and Easy Clam Cakes

Serves 3

INGREDIENTS:

- 2 6.5-ounce cans minced clams, drained and rinsed
- 1 egg, beaten
- 1 garlic clove, minced
- 1 tablespoon lemon juice
- 8–10 crushed Ritz crackers
- 2 tablespoons olive oil
- 1 bag salad spring mix

DIRECTIONS:

1. Add all ingredients (except salad mix) to a skillet and cook over medium low heat. Stir until combined.
2. Shape mixture into patties and brown patties in skillet for 8 minutes on each side.
3. Serve over salad greens.

NUTRITION FACTS

4 Servings

Amount Per Serving	
Calories	185.5
Total Fat	11 g
Saturated Fat	2 g
Polyunsaturated Fat	2 g
Monounsaturated Fat	6 g
Cholesterol	73.5 mg
Sodium	120 mg
Potassium	279 mg
Total Carbohydrates	9 g
Dietary Fiber	0.5 g
Sugars	1.5 g
Protein	13 g

SIDE DISHES

Spaghetti Squash and Corn Sauté

Serves 4

INGREDIENTS:

1 teaspoon olive oil

1 small zucchini, peeled and diced

½ spaghetti squash, peeled and diced

1 can corn kernels, drained and rinsed

1 tablespoon Italian seasoning

1 tablespoon garlic powder

Dash of salt and pepper

DIRECTIONS:

1. Heat a skillet over medium heat and add olive oil. Add the vegetables and cook for 5 minutes, or until tender.
2. Stir in the corn, and cook until heated through.
3. Mix in all spices, and stir well. Serve warm.

NUTRITION FACTS

4 Servings

Amount Per Serving	
Calories	81
Total Fat	2 g
Saturated Fat	0.5 g
Polyunsaturated Fat	0.5 g
Monounsaturated Fat	1 g
Cholesterol	0 mg
Sodium	128 mg
Potassium	307.5 mg
Total Carbohydrates	16.5 g
Dietary Fiber	3 g
Sugars	2.5 g
Protein	2 g

Southwest Stuffed Sweet Potatoes

Serves 2

INGREDIENTS:

2 large sweet potatoes
1 cup black beans, cooked
1 cup corn kernels
1 cup prepared salsa

DIRECTIONS:

1. Preheat oven to 400 degrees F. Prick the potatoes with a fork and wrap in foil. Put in the oven and bake for 45–60 minutes until they pierce easily with a fork.
2. Combine the black beans, corn, and salsa in a saucepan and heat over medium heat until warmed through.
3. When potatoes are cooked, slice them open and top them with filling.

NUTRITION FACTS

2 Servings

Amount Per Serving	
Calories	352.5
Total Fat	2 g
Saturated Fat	0.5 g
Polyunsaturated Fat	1 g
Monounsaturated Fat	0.5 g
Cholesterol	0 mg
Sodium	591.5 mg
Potassium	1,054 mg
Total Carbohydrates	74.5 g
Dietary Fiber	15.5 g
Sugars	2.5 g
Protein	14 g

Cheesy Broccoli Soup

Serves 4

INGREDIENTS:

1 10-ounce package frozen, chopped broccoli

1 10-ounce can low-sodium cream of chicken soup

1 ½ cups low-fat milk

8 ounces reduced-fat cheddar cheese, shredded

DIRECTIONS:

1. Steam broccoli according to package directions. Transfer to a soup pot.
2. Add the cream of chicken soup and milk and cook over medium low heat, stirring occasionally.
3. Add cheese and stir until melted. Add more milk to thin if desired.
4. Serve hot.

NUTRITION FACTS

4 Servings

Amount Per Serving	
Calories	224.5
Total Fat	13.5 g
Saturated Fat	6.5 g
Polyunsaturated Fat	1 g
Monounsaturated Fat	2 g
Cholesterol	39 mg
Sodium	786.5 mg
Potassium	357.5 mg
Total Carbohydrates	14 g
Dietary Fiber	2 g
Sugars	5.5 g
Protein	14 g

Green Bean Casserole

Serves 4–6

INGREDIENTS:

1 can low-sodium condensed cream of
   mushroom soup

½ cup milk

2 cans green beans, drained and rinsed

½ cup whole-wheat breadcrumbs

DIRECTIONS:

1. Preheat oven to 350 degrees F.
2. Combine all ingredients in a 2-quart casserole dish.
3. Bake for 30 minutes or until casserole is bubbly. Top with extra breadcrumbs if desired.

NUTRITION FACTS

4 Servings

Amount Per Serving	
Calories	148.5
Total Fat	3 g
Saturated Fat	1 g
Polyunsaturated Fat	1 g
Monounsaturated Fat	0.5 g
Cholesterol	5 mg
Sodium	1,049.5 mg
Potassium	394.5 mg
Total Carbohydrates	24.5 g
Dietary Fiber	4.5 g
Sugars	7 g
Protein	5 g

Honey Mustard Potato Bake

Serves 4

INGREDIENTS:

- ½ pound small red potatoes, halved
- ¼ cup onion, chopped
- ¼ cup sugar-free honey mustard salad dressing

DIRECTIONS:

1. Preheat oven to 400 degrees F. Spray a baking sheet with olive oil cooking spray.
2. Toss the ingredients together in a bowl or bag. Then, spread the potato mixture on a baking sheet.
3. Bake for 35–40 minutes, until potatoes are tender when pierced with a fork.

NUTRITION FACTS

4 Servings

Amount Per Serving	
Calories	119
Total Fat	6 g
Saturated Fat	1 g
Polyunsaturated Fat	0 g
Monounsaturated Fat	0 g
Cholesterol	5 mg
Sodium	95.5 mg
Potassium	283 mg
Total Carbohydrates	14 g
Dietary Fiber	2 g
Sugars	0.5 g
Protein	1 g

Extra Speedy Spinach

Serves 4

INGREDIENTS:

1 teaspoon olive oil

½ cup onion, chopped

½ teaspoon garlic powder

1 12-ounce bag baby spinach

DIRECTIONS:

1. Sauté all ingredients over medium heat in a large skillet. Cook until spinach is wilted, about 3 minutes.

NUTRITION FACTS

4 Servings

Amount Per Serving	
Calories	37.5
Total Fat	1 g
Saturated Fat	0 g
Polyunsaturated Fat	0 g
Monounsaturated Fat	1 g
Cholesterol	0 mg
Sodium	65.5 mg
Potassium	501.5 mg
Total Carbohydrates	4.5 g
Dietary Fiber	2.5 g
Sugars	0 g
Protein	2 g

Veggie Roast

Serves 4

INGREDIENTS:

1 tablespoon olive oil

1 bag frozen broccoli florets

1 bag bell pepper and onion mix

½ packet Italian dressing seasoning mix

DIRECTIONS:

1. Preheat oven to 400 degrees F. Spray a baking sheet with olive oil cooking spray.
2. Toss vegetables with the oil and seasoning mix and arrange in a single layer on the baking sheet.
3. Roast for 30–35 minutes until veggies are soft and lightly browned.

NUTRITION FACTS

4 Servings

Amount Per Serving	
Calories	70
Total Fat	3.5 g
Saturated Fat	0.5 g
Polyunsaturated Fat	0.5 g
Monounsaturated Fat	2.5 g
Cholesterol	0 mg
Sodium	17 mg
Potassium	177.5 mg
Total Carbohydrates	7.5 g
Dietary Fiber	2.5 g
Sugars	2.5 g
Protein	2 g

Cheesy Steamed Cauliflower

Serves 4

INGREDIENTS:

1 bag frozen cauliflower florets

½ cup non-fat milk

1 cup reduced-fat shredded cheddar or
    American cheese

DIRECTIONS:

1. Steam the cauliflower over medium heat in
   a saucepan for 8–10 minutes until tender.
   Drain water.
2. Mix in non-fat milk and cheese, stir, and
   cover until cheese is melted. Stir again until
   sauce is smooth.

NUTRITION FACTS

4 Servings

Amount Per Serving	
Calories	104
Total Fat	6 g
Saturated Fat	3.5 g
Polyunsaturated Fat	0 g
Monounsaturated Fat	0 g
Cholesterol	20.5 mg
Sodium	255.5 mg
Potassium	146.5 mg
Total Carbohydrates	4 g
Dietary Fiber	2 g
Sugars	2.5 g
Protein	9 g

Bell Peppers and Corn

Serves 4

INGREDIENTS:

½ cup onion, chopped

½ cup bell peppers, chopped

1 can corn kernels, drained and rinsed

1 teaspoon taco seasoning

DIRECTIONS:

1. Heat a large skillet over medium heat. Add onion and peppers, and cook until soft.

2. Add remaining ingredients and stir until well blended.

NUTRITION FACTS

4 Servings

Amount Per Serving	
Calories	57
Total Fat	0.5 g
Saturated Fat	0 g
Polyunsaturated Fat	0.5 g
Monounsaturated Fat	0 g
Cholesterol	0 mg
Sodium	151.5 mg
Potassium	162.5 mg
Total Carbohydrates	13 g
Dietary Fiber	1.5 g
Sugars	0.5 g
Protein	2 g

Lemon Pepper
Roasted Asparagus

Serves 4

INGREDIENTS:

- 1 large bunch asparagus
- 1 tablespoon olive oil
- 1 teaspoon lemon pepper seasoning

DIRECTIONS:

1. Preheat oven to 400 degrees F. Spray a large baking sheet with cooking spray.
2. Toss the asparagus with the oil and seasoning.
3. Roast for 10-12 minutes, until asparagus is tender.

NUTRITION FACTS

4 Servings

Amount Per Serving	
Calories	62
Total Fat	3.5 g
Saturated Fat	0.5 g
Polyunsaturated Fat	0.5 g
Monounsaturated Fat	2.5 g
Cholesterol	0 mg
Sodium	3 mg
Potassium	392 mg
Total Carbohydrates	6.5 g
Dietary Fiber	3 g
Sugars	0 g
Protein	3 g

Balsamic Lacquered Beets

Serves 6

INGREDIENTS:

¼ cup sugar blend for baking

1 tablespoon cornstarch

Pinch of salt

½ cup olive oil

½ cup balsamic vinegar

3 15-ounce cans sliced beets, drained and rinsed

DIRECTIONS:

1. In a small bowl, combine sugar blend, cornstarch, and salt.

2. In a saucepan over medium heat, cook oil and vinegar. Add sugar blend mixture and stir constantly.

3. Add beets to saucepan. Cover and cook for 15 minutes.

NUTRITION FACTS

6 Servings

Amount Per Serving	
Calories	281.5
Total Fat	18 g
Saturated Fat	2.5 g
Polyunsaturated Fat	1.5 g
Monounsaturated Fat	13.5 g
Cholesterol	0 mg
Sodium	540 mg
Potassium	0 mg
Total Carbohydrates	25 g
Dietary Fiber	1.5 g
Sugars	18 g
Protein	0 g

Citrus Orzo

Serves 4

INGREDIENTS:

1 cup dry orzo pasta (about 6 ounces)

2 tablespoons lemon juice

Dash of salt and pepper

1 teaspoon basil

1 teaspoon thyme

½ cup reduced-fat Parmesan cheese

DIRECTIONS

1. Cook pasta in a medium saucepan according to package directions. Drain.
2. Add remaining ingredients to saucepan and stir. Serve warm.

NUTRITION FACTS

4 Servings

Amount Per Serving	
Calories	258.5
Total Fat	5 g
Saturated Fat	2.5 g
Polyunsaturated Fat	0 g
Monounsaturated Fat	1 g
Cholesterol	10 mg
Sodium	234.5 mg
Potassium	21 mg
Total Carbohydrates	43 g
Dietary Fiber	2 g
Sugars	1 g
Protein	12 g

Herbed Roasted Vegetables

Serves 4

INGREDIENTS:

2 carrots, cut into 1-inch chunks

1 bag frozen Brussels sprouts, thawed

1 medium red onion, quartered

1 tablespoon olive oil

2 cloves garlic, minced

1 teaspoon thyme

1 teaspoon rosemary

Dash of salt and pepper

DIRECTIONS:

1. Preheat oven to 425 degrees F. Place carrots, Brussels sprouts, and red onion in a 13 x 9 inch baking pan coated in olive oil cooking spray.

2. In a small bowl, mix together oil, garlic, herbs, salt, and pepper. Pour over vegetables.

3. Bake for 35 minutes or until vegetables are tender and lightly browned.

NUTRITION FACTS

4 Servings

Amount Per Serving	
Calories	106
Total Fat	3.5 g
Saturated Fat	0.5 g
Polyunsaturated Fat	0.5 g
Monounsaturated Fat	2.5 g
Cholesterol	0 mg
Sodium	41 mg
Potassium	180 mg
Total Carbohydrates	15 g
Dietary Fiber	4.5 g
Sugars	3.5 g
Protein	4 g

Warm Cabbage and Onion Salad

Serves 4

INGREDIENTS:

1 ½ tablespoons olive oil

1 medium onion, chopped

½ bag coleslaw mix (7 ounces)

1 tablespoon low-sodium soy sauce

Dash of pepper

DIRECTIONS:

1. Heat the oil over medium-high heat in a skillet. Add onion, and cook until soft.

2. Add the cabbage and cook 3–5 minutes so that the cabbage is softened but maintains some crispness. Add soy sauce and pepper. Serve warm.

NUTRITION FACTS

4 Servings

Amount Per Serving	
Calories	31
Total Fat	1.5 g
Saturated Fat	0 g
Polyunsaturated Fat	0 g
Monounsaturated Fat	1.5 g
Cholesterol	0 mg
Sodium	146.5 mg
Potassium	43 mg
Total Carbohydrates	3 g
Dietary Fiber	0.5 g
Sugars	0.5 g
Protein	0.5 g

Creamy Peas

Serves 4

INGREDIENTS:

1 bag frozen peas

¼ cup non-fat sour cream

1 green onion, chopped

DIRECTIONS:

1. Cook peas according to bag directions.
2. Stir in sour cream and green onion while peas are still warm.

Amount Per Serving	
Calories	76
Total Fat	0.5 g
Saturated Fat	0 g
Polyunsaturated Fat	0 g
Monounsaturated Fat	0.0 g
Cholesterol	1.5 mg
Sodium	91.5 mg
Potassium	168.5 mg
Total Carbohydrates	13.5 g
Dietary Fiber	3.5 g
Sugars	5 g
Protein	4.5 g

Parmesan and Parsley Tomatoes

Serves 4

INGREDIENTS:

¼ cup light mayonnaise

¼ cup grated reduced-fat Parmesan cheese

1 tablespoon parsley

3 small tomatoes, halved

DIRECTIONS:

1. Preheat broiler. Combine the first 3 ingredients in a small bowl until fully combined.
2. Spoon mixture onto tomato halves. Broil 4 inches from heat source for 3–4 minutes, or until lightly browned.

NUTRITION FACTS

4 Servings

Amount Per Serving	
Calories	77
Total Fat	5 g
Saturated Fat	1 g
Polyunsaturated Fat	2 g
Monounsaturated Fat	1 g
Cholesterol	4 mg
Sodium	196.5 mg
Potassium	218 mg
Total Carbohydrates	6.5 g
Dietary Fiber	1 g
Sugars	1 g
Protein	3 g

Fresh Cucumber Salad

Serves 4

INGREDIENTS:

2 cucumbers, thinly sliced

½ medium sweet onion, thinly sliced

1 teaspoon dried dill

1 tablespoon olive oil

1 tablespoon lemon juice

1 tablespoon white-wine vinegar

Dash of salt and pepper

DIRECTIONS:

1. In a freezer bag, toss together all ingredients. Serve chilled.

NUTRITION FACTS

4 Servings

Amount Per Serving	
Calories	56
Total Fat	3.5 g
Saturated Fat	0.5 g
Polyunsaturated Fat	0.5 g
Monounsaturated Fat	2.5 g
Cholesterol	0 mg
Sodium	4 mg
Potassium	242 mg
Total Carbohydrates	5.5 g
Dietary Fiber	1.5 g
Sugars	0 g
Protein	1 g

Beef and Broccoli Stir Fry, *page 80*

Best Roasted Chicken, *page 65* 149

Seafood Corn Chowder, *page 107*

Split Pea Soup, *page 108*

Italian Zucchini Bake, *page 41*

Cream Corn Casserole, *page 44*

Fresh Cucumber Salad, *page 144*

Greek Salad, *page 161*

Applesauce Cake, *page 237*

30-Second Brownies, *page 244*

Greek Salad

Serves 8

INGREDIENTS:

- 1 head Romaine lettuce or 1 bag lettuce mix
- 4 tomatoes, chopped
- 1 cucumber, sliced
- 1 (4-ounce) can black olives, drained and rinsed
- ½ cup feta cheese
- 2 cups sugar-free Greek dressing

DIRECTIONS:

1. Tear lettuce into small pieces. Place lettuce, tomatoes, cucumber, olives, and feta cheese in a large serving bowl and toss.
2. Drizzle with dressing and serve.

NUTRITION FACTS

8 Servings

Amount Per Serving	
Calories	178
Total Fat	15.5 g
Saturated Fat	3.5 g
Polyunsaturated Fat	0.5 g
Monounsaturated Fat	1 g
Cholesterol	8.5 mg
Sodium	681 mg
Potassium	279 mg
Total Carbohydrates	7.5 g
Dietary Fiber	2 g
Sugars	0 g
Protein	2.5 g

Citrus and Almonds Salad

Serves 4

INGREDIENTS:

- 1 bag spring mix salad
- 1 can mandarin orange segments, drained and rinsed
- ¼ cup almonds, sliced
- 1 tablespoon sugar-free orange marmalade
- 2 tablespoons red wine vinegar
- ¼ cup olive oil

DIRECTIONS:

1. Empty salad mix into a large bowl. Add in orange segments and almonds, and toss everything together.
2. In a small bowl, prepare the vinaigrette dressing by whisking together the marmalade, red wine vinegar, and olive oil.

NUTRITION FACTS

4 Servings

Amount Per Serving	
Calories	192.5
Total Fat	17.5 g
Saturated Fat	2 g
Polyunsaturated Fat	1 g
Monounsaturated Fat	10 g
Cholesterol	0 mg
Sodium	40 mg
Potassium	124.5 mg
Total Carbohydrates	8.5 g
Dietary Fiber	2.5 g
Sugars	4 g
Protein	3 g

Couscous Pilaf

Serves 6

INGREDIENTS:

  2 cups low-sodium chicken broth
  1 (10-ounce) package uncooked couscous
  ¼ cup grated Parmesan cheese
  1 tablespoon fresh lemon juice
  1 teaspoon oregano

DIRECTIONS:

1. In a medium saucepan, bring 2 cups chicken broth to a boil. Stir in couscous, cover, and remove from heat. Let stand 5 minutes.
2. Stir in Parmesan cheese, lemon juice, and oregano.
3. Fluff with a fork and serve.

NUTRITION FACTS

6 Servings

Amount Per Serving	
Calories	78
Total Fat	1.5 g
Saturated Fat	0.5 g
Polyunsaturated Fat	0 g
Monounsaturated Fat	0.5 g
Cholesterol	2.5 mg
Sodium	219.5 mg
Potassium	91 mg
Total Carbohydrate	33.5 g
Dietary Fiber	2 g
Sugars	0 g
Protein	7 g

Cauliflower and Rice Casserole

Serves 10

INGREDIENTS:

- 2 (10.5-ounce) cans low-sodium condensed cream of broccoli soup
- 1 cup low-fat milk
- 1 bag frozen chopped cauliflower, thawed
- 1 cup cooked brown rice
- 1 small onion, chopped
- 1 cup reduced-fat shredded Mexican cheese blend, divided

DIRECTIONS:

1. Preheat oven to 350 degrees F. Combine all ingredients in 9 x 9 inch baking dish coated with olive oil cooking spray.
2. Bake 15 minutes. Stir. Bake for an additional 15 minutes.

NUTRITION FACTS

10 Servings

Amount Per Serving	
Calories	98.5
Total Fat	3.5 g
Saturated Fat	2 g
Polyunsaturated Fat	0 g
Monounsaturated Fat	0.5 g
Cholesterol	8.5 mg
Sodium	285.5 mg
Potassium	151 mg
Total Carbohydrates	11.5 g
Dietary Fiber	2 g
Sugars	1.5 g
Protein	5.5 g

Brown Rice with Mushrooms

Serves 4

INGREDIENTS:

½ tablespoon olive oil

1 small onion, diced

6 large mushrooms, chopped

¾ cup brown rice

1 ¾ cups low sodium vegetable broth

Salt and pepper to taste

DIRECTIONS:

1. In a small saucepan, cook onions in oil over medium heat until onions are soft.
2. Add mushrooms, and cook 5 minutes, stirring intermittently.
3. Add in brown rice and allow to cook for 3 minutes. Stir in vegetable broth and cover.
4. Reduce heat to low and let simmer for 30–40 minutes or until the rice absorbs most of the liquid. Add salt and pepper to taste.

NUTRITION FACTS

4 Servings

Amount Per Serving	
Calories	172
Total Fat	3 g
Saturated Fat	0.5 g
Polyunsaturated Fat	0 g
Monounsaturated Fat	1 g
Cholesterol	0 mg
Sodium	64.5 mg
Potassium	232 mg
Total Carbohydrates	32 g
Dietary Fiber	3.5 g
Sugars	1.5 g
Protein	4 g

Black Bean Salad

Serves 4

INGREDIENTS:

3 tablespoons fresh lime juice

Pinch of crushed red pepper flakes

1 15-ounce can black beans, drained and rinsed

1 cup canned chickpeas, drained and rinsed

1 cup cherry tomatoes, quartered

DIRECTIONS:

1. In a large bowl, combine all ingredients and toss to coat with lime juice. Serve chilled.

NUTRITION FACTS

4 Servings

Amount Per Serving	
Calories	165.5
Total Fat	1 g
Saturated Fat	0 g
Polyunsaturated Fat	0.5 g
Monounsaturated Fat	0 g
Cholesterol	0 mg
Sodium	364 mg
Potassium	590 mg
Total Carbohydrates	35 g
Dietary Fiber	7.5 g
Sugars	1 g
Protein	8.5 g

Cauliflower Mashed "Potatoes"

Serves 4

INGREDIENTS:

- 1 bag frozen cauliflower or 1 head fresh cauliflower
- 1/3 cup low-fat milk
- 1 teaspoon lemon juice
- 1 teaspoon garlic powder
- 1 teaspoons olive oil
- Salt and pepper to taste

DIRECTIONS:

1. Steam cauliflower in a saucepan until it is extra soft, about 10–15 minutes.
2. Place cauliflower in a food processor and process until pasty. Add in remaining ingredients and pulse until smooth. Serve warm.

NUTRITION FACTS

4 Servings

Amount Per Serving	
Calories	54.5
Total Fat	1.5 g
Saturated Fat	0.5 g
Polyunsaturated Fat	0 g
Monounsaturated Fat	1 g
Cholesterol	1 mg
Sodium	52 mg
Potassium	466 mg
Total Carbohydrates	8.5 g
Dietary Fiber 3.6 g	0 g
Sugars 1.0 g	0 g
Protein 3.5 g	0 g

DESSERTS

Birthday Cake

Serves 2

INGREDIENTS:

- 4 tablespoons self-rising flour
- 4 tablespoons sugar blend
- 2 tablespoons beaten egg or liquid egg substitute
- 3 tablespoons milk
- 2 tablespoons vegetable oil
- ½ teaspoon vanilla extract
- 1 teaspoon rainbow sprinkles

DIRECTIONS:

1. Mix flour and sugar together in a small bowl. Add egg or egg substitute, milk, oil, and extract, and mix until fully combined.

2. Divide between two small mugs. Microwave on high for 1 minute, or until top of mug cakes are dry. Top with sprinkles.

NUTRITION FACTS

2 Servings

Amount Per Serving	
Calories	202.5
Total Fat	15 g
Saturated Fat	10.5 g
Polyunsaturated Fat	0 g
Monounsaturated Fat	0 g
Cholesterol	2.5 mg
Sodium	42 mg
Potassium	77.5 mg
Total Carbohydrate	13.5 g
Dietary Fiber	0.5 g
Sugars	2 g
Protein	4 g

Coconut Lime Cake

Serves 2

INGREDIENTS:

- 4 tablespoons self-rising flour
- 2 ½ tablespoons sugar blend
- 4 tablespoons full-fat coconut milk
- ½ teaspoon vanilla extract
- 1 tablespoon shredded coconut
- ¼ teaspoon lime zest

DIRECTIONS:

1. Mix flour and sugar together in a small bowl.
2. Add coconut milk and vanilla extract, and mix until fully combined.
3. Stir in coconut and lime zest.
4. Divide between two small mugs. Microwave on high for 1 minute, or until top of mug cakes are dry.

NUTRITION FACTS

2 Servings

Amount Per Serving	
Calories	138
Total Fat	4.5 g
Saturated Fat	3 g
Polyunsaturated Fat	0 g
Monounsaturated Fat	0 g
Cholesterol	0 g
Sodium	65 mg
Potassium	6 mg
Total Carbohydrate	19.5 g
Dietary Fiber	0.5 g
Sugars	15.5 g
Protein	1 g

Oatmeal Apple Cake

Serves 2

INGREDIENTS:

1 packet instant plain oatmeal

1 tablespoon brown sugar blend

2 tablespoons self-rising flour

3 tablespoons milk

1 tablespoon olive oil

1/3 apple, diced

DIRECTIONS:

1. Mix all ingredients, except the apple, together in a small bowl. Divide between two small mugs.

2. Microwave on High for 1 minute.

3. Top with fresh apple.

NUTRITION FACTS

2 Servings

Amount Per Serving	
Calories	216
Total Fat	8.5 g
Saturated Fat	1.5 g
Polyunsaturated Fat	1 g
Monounsaturated Fat	5 g
Cholesterol	3.5 mg
Sodium	154.5 mg
Potassium	50 mg
Total Carbohydrate	33.5 g
Dietary Fiber	3 g
Sugars	15.5 g
Protein	4 g

Banana Raisin Cake

Serves 2

INGREDIENTS:

4 tablespoons self-rising flour

4 tablespoons brown sugar blend

2 tablespoons beaten egg or liquid egg substitute

3 tablespoons milk

2 tablespoons vegetable oil

½ ripe banana, mashed

1–2 tablespoons raisins

DIRECTIONS:

1. Mix flour and sugar together in a small bowl. Add egg, milk, oil, and banana, and mix until fully combined. Stir in raisins.

2. Divide between two small mugs. Microwave on high for 1 minute, or until top of mug cakes are dry.

NUTRITION FACTS

2 Servings

Amount Per Serving	
Calories	287.5
Total Fat	15 g
Saturated Fat	10.5 g
Polyunsaturated Fat	0 g
Monounsaturated Fat	0 g
Cholesterol	2.5 mg
Sodium	40.5 mg
Potassium	234 mg
Total Carbohydrate	36.5 g
Dietary Fiber	1.5 g
Sugars	21 g
Protein	4.5 g

Cheesecake for Two

Serves 2

INGREDIENTS:

Crust

2 graham crackers, crushed

1 tablespoon unsalted butter, melted

Cake

4 tablespoons reduced-fat cream cheese

2 tablespoons plain Greek yogurt

2 ½ tablespoons sugar or sugar substitute

1 egg

½ teaspoon vanilla extract

DIRECTIONS:

1. Mix the graham cracker crumbs and melted butter together. Press the mixture into the bottom of two small mugs.

2. In a small bowl, whisk together all cake ingredients until smooth, divide, and pour into mugs.

3. Microwave 2 ½ minutes until centers are set. Allow cakes to cool, and then refrigerate for 2 hours.

NUTRITION FACTS

2 Servings

Amount Per Serving	
Calories	231.5
Total Fat	15 g
Saturated Fat	8 g
Polyunsaturated Fat	1.5 g
Monounsaturated Fat	4 g
Cholesterol	126 mg
Sodium	233.5 mg
Potassium	108 mg
Total Carbohydrate	15.5 g
Dietary Fiber	1 g
Sugars	5 g
Protein	8 g

Carrot Cake with Raisins

Serves 2

INGREDIENTS:

4 tablespoons self-rising flour

Sugar substitute equal to 4 tablespoons sugar

⅛ teaspoon cinnamon

⅛ teaspoon nutmeg

¼ cup canned carrots, drained, rinsed,
    and mashed

2 tablespoons beaten egg or liquid egg substitute

3 tablespoons milk

2 tablespoons vegetable oil

2 tablespoons raisins

DIRECTIONS:

1. Mix flour, sugar, cinnamon, and nutmeg together in a small bowl.
2. Add all wet ingredients and mix until fully combined. Stir in raisins.
3. Divide between two small mugs. Microwave on high for 1 minute, or until top of mug cakes are dry.

NUTRITION FACTS

2 Servings

Amount Per Serving	
Calories	220
Total Fat	15 g
Saturated Fat	10.5 g
Polyunsaturated Fat	0 g
Monounsaturated Fat	0 g
Cholesterol	2.5 mg
Sodium	51.5 mg
Potassium	174.5 mg
Total Carbohydrate	19.5 g
Dietary Fiber	1.5 g
Sugars	6 g
Protein	4.5 g

Cranberry Orange Cake

Serves 2

INGREDIENTS:

4 tablespoons self-rising flour

Sugar substitute equal to 4 tablespoons sugar

2 tablespoons beaten egg or liquid egg substitute

3 tablespoons milk

2 tablespoons vegetable oil

1 tablespoon cranberry sauce

1 tablespoon orange juice

⅛ teaspoon orange extract

1 handful dried cranberries or cranberry-raisins

DIRECTIONS:

1. Mix flour and sugar in a small bowl. Add egg, milk, oil, cranberry sauce, orange juice, and orange extract, and stir until well combined.
2. Mix in dried cranberries.
3. Divide between two small mugs. Microwave on High for 1 minute or until tops are dry.

NUTRITION FACTS

2 Servings

Amount Per Serving	
Calories	257.5
Total Fat	15 g
Saturated Fat	10.5 g
Polyunsaturated Fat	0 g
Monounsaturated Fat	0 g
Cholesterol	2.5 mg
Sodium	41 mg
Potassium	97 mg
Total Carbohydrate	29.5 g
Dietary Fiber	1.5 g
Sugars	15 g
Protein	4 g

Blueberry Peach Cake

Serves 2

INGREDIENTS:

4 tablespoons self-rising flour

Sugar substitute equal to 4 tablespoons sugar

2 tablespoons beaten egg or liquid egg substitute

3 tablespoons milk

2 tablespoons vegetable oil

¼ teaspoon vanilla

¼ cup blueberries

¼ cup diced peaches

DIRECTIONS:

1. Mix the flour and sugar together in a small bowl. Add the egg, milk, oil, and vanilla, and stir until well-combined. Fold in the fruit.

2. Divide into two small mugs. Microwave on High for 1 minute or until the tops are dry.

NUTRITION FACTS

2 Servings

Amount Per Serving	
Calories	211.5
Total Fat	15 g
Saturated Fat	10.5 g
Polyunsaturated Fat	0 g
Monounsaturated Fat	0 g
Cholesterol	2.5 mg
Sodium	40.5 mg
Potassium	134 mg
Total Carbohydrate	17g
Dietary Fiber	1.5 g
Sugars	5 g
Protein	4 g

Mint Chocolate Pudding

Serves 2

INGREDIENTS:

1 tablespoon cornstarch

2 tablespoons cocoa powder

Sugar substitute equal to 3 tablespoons sugar

¾ cup hot milk

¼ teaspoon mint extract

DIRECTIONS:

1. Mix the cornstarch, cocoa powder, and sugar together in a small bowl. Add the warm milk and mint extract.
2. Divide between two small mugs. Microwave on High for 1 minute or until the tops are dry.

NUTRITION FACTS

2 Servings

Amount Per Serving	
Calories	172
Total Fat	3.5 g
Saturated Fat	2 g
Polyunsaturated Fat	0 g
Monounsaturated Fat	1 g
Cholesterol	9 mg
Sodium	38 mg
Potassium	213.5 mg
Total Carbohydrate	28.5 g
Dietary Fiber	2 g
Sugars	23 g
Protein	4 g

Cherry Cobbler

Serves 2

INGREDIENTS:

2 tablespoons quick-cooking oats

1 tablespoon brown sugar blend

1 tablespoon all-purpose flour

1 tablespoon cold unsalted butter

¼ teaspoon vanilla extract

½ cup fresh or frozen cherries, thawed

DIRECTIONS:

1. Mix together oats, brown sugar, and flour in a small bowl.

2. Press down on the butter with a fork until it crumbles. Add butter to mixture. Add fruit.

3. Divide between two small mugs. Microwave on high for 1 minute, or until fruit bubbles. Stir before serving.

NUTRITION FACTS

2 Servings

Amount Per Serving	
Calories	243.5
Total Fat	12 g
Saturated Fat	7.5 g
Polyunsaturated Fat	0.5 g
Monounsaturated Fat	3.5 g
Cholesterol	31 mg
Sodium	22.5 mg
Potassium	196.5 mg
Total Carbohydrate	32.5 g
Dietary Fiber	2.5 g
Sugars	21.5 g
Protein	2.5 g

Banana French Toast

Serves 2

INGREDIENTS:

2 slices wheat bread, cubed

1 egg or egg substitute

4 tablespoons milk

¼ banana, mashed

⅛ teaspoon vanilla extract

⅛ teaspoon cinnamon

1 teaspoon sugar-free pancake syrup,
   for drizzling

DIRECTIONS:

1. Place cubes of bread in the bottom of two small mugs.

2. In a small bowl, whisk together the egg and milk. Add banana, vanilla, and cinnamon to egg mixture. Pour into mugs and wait to allow bread to soak up liquid.

3. Microwave on High for 1–1 ½ minutes. Drizzle with maple syrup.

NUTRITION FACTS

2 Servings

Amount Per Serving	
Calories	151.5
Total Fat	4.5 g
Saturated Fat	1.5 g
Polyunsaturated Fat	1 g
Monounsaturated Fat	1 g
Cholesterol	96 mg
Sodium	151.5 mg
Potassium	159.5 mg
Total Carbohydrate	19.5 g
Dietary Fiber	2.5 g
Sugars	7.5 g
Protein	8 g

Chocolate Chip Muffin Cake

Serves 2

INGREDIENTS:

4 tablespoons self-rising flour

Sugar substitute equal to 4 tablespoons sugar

2 tablespoons beaten egg or liquid egg substitute

3 tablespoons milk

2 tablespoons vegetable oil

1 handful semi-sweet chocolate chips

DIRECTIONS:

1. Mix flour and sugar together in a small bowl. Whisk together egg, milk, and vegetable oil until fully combined. Stir in chocolate chips.

2. Divide between two small mugs. Microwave on high for 1 minute, or until top of mug cakes are dry.

NUTRITION FACTS

2 Servings

Amount Per Serving	
Calories	297
Total Fat	21.5 g
Saturated Fat	15 g
Polyunsaturated Fat	0 g
Monounsaturated Fat	0 g
Cholesterol	2.5 mg
Sodium	46.5 mg
Potassium	76 mg
Total Carbohydrate	26 g
Dietary Fiber	2 g
Sugars	11.5 g
Protein	4 g

Caramel Pecan Cake

Serves 2

INGREDIENTS:

4 tablespoons self-rising flour

Sugar substitute equal to 4 tablespoons sugar

2 tablespoons beaten egg or liquid egg substitute

3 tablespoons milk

2 tablespoons vegetable oil

½ teaspoon vanilla extract

1 handful pecans

1 tablespoon sugar-free caramel sauce

DIRECTIONS:

1. Mix flour and sugar together in a small bowl.

2. Whisk together egg, milk, oil, and vanilla extract until fully combined. Stir in pecans. Divide this mixture between two small mugs.

3. Microwave on high for 1 minute, or until top of mug cakes are dry. Drizzle with caramel sauce and serve.

NUTRITION FACTS

2 Servings

Amount Per Serving	
Calories	323
Total Fat	26 g
Saturated Fat	11.5 g
Polyunsaturated Fat	3.5 g
Monounsaturated Fat	6.5 g
Cholesterol	3.5 mg
Sodium	51.8 mg
Potassium	138.5 mg
Total Carbohydrate	19.5 g
Dietary Fiber	1.9 g
Sugars	1.9 g
Protein	5.3 g

Cran-Apple Walnut Crunch Cake

Serves 16

INGREDIENTS:

- 2 (21-ounce) cans no-sugar-added apple pie filling
- 1 can whole-berry cranberry sauce
- 1 box sugar-free yellow cake mix
- 1 can cranberry seltzer (12 ounces)
- 1 cup walnuts, chopped

DIRECTIONS:

1. Preheat the oven to 350 degrees F. Grease a 9 x 13 inch baking dish with light cooking spray.

2. Spread the pie filling over the bottom of the baking dish. Spread cranberry sauce over the pie filling.

3. Sprinkle the cake mix onto the cranberry sauce. Pour seltzer over cake mix.

4. Sprinkle on walnuts.

5. Bake for 35–40 minutes or until fruit is bubbly.

NUTRITION FACTS

16 Servings

Amount Per Serving	
Calories	278.5
Total Fat	8.5 g
Saturated Fat	1.5 g
Polyunsaturated Fat	3.5 g
Monounsaturated Fat	0.5 g
Cholesterol	0 mg
Sodium	220 mg
Potassium	42 mg
Total Carbohydrate	36.5 g
Dietary Fiber	1 g
Sugars	13.5 g
Protein	2 g

Easy Apple Peach Cake

Serves 16

INGREDIENTS:

1 (21-ounce) can no-sugar-added
    apple pie filling

1 (21-ounce) can peach pie filling

1 box sugar-free yellow cake mix

1 can peach-flavored seltzer water (12 ounces)

DIRECTIONS:

1. Preheat the oven to 350 degrees F. Grease
   a 9 x 13 inch baking dish with light
   cooking spray.

2. Spread the pie filling over the bottom of the
   baking dish. Sprinkle the cake mix over the
   fruit. Pour seltzer over the cake mix. Bake
   for 35–40 minutes or until fruit is bubbly.

NUTRITION FACTS

16 Servings

Amount Per Serving	
Calories	199.5
Total Fat	3 g
Saturated Fat	1 g
Polyunsaturated Fat	0 g
Monounsaturated Fat	0 g
Cholesterol	0 mg
Sodium	216.5 mg
Potassium	0 mg
Total Carbohydrate	33 g
Dietary Fiber	1 g
Sugars	9 g
Protein	1 g

Choco-Raspberry Dump Cake

Serves 12

INGREDIENTS:

2 (12-ounce) bags frozen raspberries

1 box sugar-free chocolate cake mix

1 can diet cherry soda

DIRECTIONS:

1. Preheat oven to 350 degrees F. Spray a 9 x 13 inch dish with light cooking spray.

2. Cover bottom of cake dish with fruit. Sprinkle cake mix over the fruit.

3. Pour soda over cake mix, being sure to moisten as much of the mix as possible.

4. Bake 35–45 minutes, or until fruit is bubbly.

NUTRITION FACTS

12 Servings

Amount Per Serving	
Calories	131.5
Total Fat	3.5 g
Saturated Fat	1.5 g
Polyunsaturated Fat	0 g
Monounsaturated Fat	0 g
Cholesterol	0 mg
Sodium	254.5 mg
Potassium	35 mg
Total Carbohydrate	32 g
Dietary Fiber	2.5 g
Sugars	1 g
Protein	2.5 g

Ginger Spiced Pear Cake

Serves 12

INGREDIENTS:

2 (15-ounce) cans sliced pears, drained

1 box sugar-free gingerbread cake mix

1 (12-ounce) can diet ginger ale

DIRECTIONS:

1. Preheat oven to 350 degrees F. Spray a 9 x 13 inch dish with light cooking spray.
2. Cover bottom of cake dish with fruit. Sprinkle cake mix over the fruit.
3. Pour soda over cake mix, being sure to moisten as much of the mix as possible.
4. Bake 35–45 minutes, or until fruit is bubbly.

NUTRITION FACTS

12 Servings

Amount Per Serving	
Calories	145
Total Fat	3.5 g
Saturated Fat	1.5 g
Polyunsaturated Fat	0 g
Monounsaturated Fat	0 g
Cholesterol	0 mg
Sodium	291.5 mg
Potassium	40 mg
Total Carbohydrate	35 g
Dietary Fiber	1 g
Sugars	6 g
Protein	1 g

Lemon Strawberry Dump Cake

Serves 16

INGREDIENTS:

2 (14-ounce) bags frozen sliced strawberries

Zest of one lemon

1 box sugar-free yellow cake mix

1 can diet lemon-lime soda

DIRECTIONS:

1. Preheat oven to 350 degrees F. Spray a 9 x 13 inch dish with light cooking spray.
2. Cover bottom of cake dish with fruit. Sprinkle zest and cake mix over the fruit.
3. Pour soda over cake mix, being sure to moisten as much of the mix as possible.
4. Bake 35–45 minutes, or until fruit is bubbly.

NUTRITION FACTS

16 Servings

Amount Per Serving	
Calories	101
Total Fat	2.5 g
Saturated Fat	1 g
Polyunsaturated Fat	0 g
Monounsaturated Fat	0 g
Cholesterol	0 mg
Sodium	212.5 mg
Potassium	0.5 mg
Total Carbohydrate	24.5 g
Dietary Fiber	1 g
Sugars	1.5 g
Protein	1 g

Raspberry Cream Cheesecake

Serves 10

INGREDIENTS:

1 (8-ounce) container reduced-fat cream cheese,
   room temperature

1 (10-ounce) jar sugar-free raspberry jelly

½ teaspoon vanilla extract

½ container light whipped topping, thawed

1 ready-made reduced-fat graham cracker crust

DIRECTIONS:

1. In a large bowl, use an electric mixer to
    combine cream cheese, raspberry jam, and
    vanilla. Add in cool whip and mix by hand.

2. Pour into pie crust and chill in refrigerator
    until set.

NUTRITION FACTS

10 Servings

Amount Per Serving	
Calories	208
Total Fat	11 g
Saturated Fat	5.5 g
Polyunsaturated Fat	1.5 g
Monounsaturated Fat	3.5 g
Cholesterol	13.5 mg
Sodium	199 mg
Potassium	59 mg
Total Carbohydrate	26.5 g
Dietary Fiber	0.5 g
Sugars	11.5 g
Protein	3.5 g

Pistachio Cake

Serves 16

INGREDIENTS:

1 box sugar-free pistachio instant pudding mix

1 ½ cups milk

1 box sugar-free yellow cake mix

1 cup pistachios or walnuts, chopped

DIRECTIONS:

1. Preheat the oven to 350 degrees F. Spray a 9 x 13 inch baking dish with light cooking spray.

2. Whisk together the pudding mix and the milk until pudding forms. Add in the dry cake mix, and stir until combined.

3. Pour the batter into the prepared baking dish and sprinkle the nuts on top.

4. Bake for 30 minutes or until a toothpick inserted into the center of the cake comes out clean.

NUTRITION FACTS

16 Servings

Amount Per Serving	
Calories	154
Total Fat	7 g
Saturated Fat	2 g
Polyunsaturated Fat	1 g
Monounsaturated Fat	2 g
Cholesterol	2.5 mg
Sodium	296.5 mg
Potassium	114.5 mg
Total Carbohydrate	26.5 g
Dietary Fiber	1 g
Sugars	2 g
Protein	3 g

Chocolate Marshmallow Cake

Serves 16

INGREDIENTS:

1 box sugar-free instant chocolate pudding mix

1 ½ cups milk

1 box sugar-free Devil's food cake mix

⅔ cup miniature marshmallows

DIRECTIONS:

1. Preheat the oven to 350 degrees F. Spray a 9 x 13 inch baking dish with light cooking spray.

2. Whisk together the chocolate pudding mix and the milk until pudding forms. Add in the dry cake mix, and mix until combined. Stir in marshmallows.

3. Bake for 30 minutes or until a toothpick inserted into the center of the cake comes out clean.

NUTRITION FACTS

16 Servings

Amount Per Serving	
Calories	118.5
Total Fat	3.5 g
Saturated Fat	1.5 g
Polyunsaturated Fat	0 g
Monounsaturated Fat	0 g
Cholesterol	2.5 mg
Sodium	275.5 mg
Potassium	32.5 mg
Total Carbohydrate	26.5 g
Dietary Fiber	1 g
Sugars	2.5 g
Protein	2.5 g

Dark Chocolate Walnut Cake

Serves 16

INGREDIENTS:

1 box instant sugar-free chocolate pudding mix

1 ½ cups milk

1 box sugar-free Devil's food cake mix

¾ cup walnuts, chopped

¼ cup dark chocolate chips

DIRECTIONS:

1. Preheat the oven to 350 degrees F. Spray a 9 x 13 inch baking dish with light cooking spray.
2. Whisk together the chocolate pudding mix and the milk until pudding forms. Add in the dry cake mix, and stir until combined.
3. Pour the batter into the prepared baking dish and sprinkle the almonds and chocolate chips on top.
4. Bake for 30 minutes or until a toothpick inserted into the center of the cake comes out clean.

NUTRITION FACTS

16 Servings

Amount Per Serving	
Calories	160
Total Fat	8 g
Saturated Fat	2.5 g
Polyunsaturated Fat	2.5 g
Monounsaturated Fat	0.5 g
Cholesterol	2.5 mg
Sodium	217.5 mg
Potassium	57.5 mg
Total Carbohydrate	26.5 g
Dietary Fiber	1.5 g
Sugars	3 g
Protein	3 g

Chocolate Cream Pie

Serves 10

INGREDIENTS:

- 1 box sugar-free instant chocolate pudding mix
- 1 ½ cups milk
- 1 cup fat-free sour cream
- 1 ready-made graham cracker pie crust

DIRECTIONS:

1. In a medium-sized bowl, prepare pudding by whisking together pudding mix and milk. Add in sour cream, and mix until well combined.
2. Pour into pie crust and refrigerate until set.

NUTRITION FACTS

10 Servings

Amount Per Serving	
Calories	184.5
Total Fat	6.5 g
Saturated Fat	1.5 g
Polyunsaturated Fat	1.5 g
Monounsaturated Fat	3 g
Cholesterol	2 mg
Sodium	482.5 mg
Potassium	76 mg
Total Carbohydrate	28 g
Dietary Fiber	1.5 g
Sugars	12.5 g
Protein	4 g

Taste of the Tropics Cake

Serves 16

INGREDIENTS:

2 (20-ounce) cans no-sugar-added crushed
   pineapple, drained

½ cup shredded coconut

1 box sugar-free yellow cake mix

1 can diet lemon-lime soda

DIRECTIONS:

1. Preheat the oven to 350 degrees F. Spray
   a 9 x 13 inch baking dish with light
   cooking spray.

2. Pour pineapple into the bottom of the
   prepared baking dish. Sprinkle shredded
   coconut and cake mix evenly over pineapple.
   Pour soda over cake mix, being sure to
   moisten as much of the mix as possible.

3. Bake for 35–40 minutes or until fruit is hot
   and bubbly.

NUTRITION FACTS

16 Servings

Amount Per Serving	
Calories	151.5
Total Fat	4 g
Saturated Fat	1 g
Polyunsaturated Fat	0 g
Monounsaturated Fat	0 g
Cholesterol	0 mg
Sodium	220 mg
Potassium	94 mg
Total Carbohydrate	33.5 g
Dietary Fiber	1.5 g
Sugars	9.5 g
Protein	1.5 g

Orange Mango Cake

Serves 12

INGREDIENTS:

- 1 (20-ounce) can no-sugar-added sliced peaches, drained
- 1 (15-ounce) can no-sugar-added diced mangoes, drained
- 1 box sugar-free yellow cake mix
- 1 can orange seltzer

DIRECTIONS:

1. Preheat the oven to 350 degrees F. Spray a 9 x 13 inch baking dish with light cooking spray.

2. Pour peaches and mangoes into the bottom of the prepared baking dish. Sprinkle cake mix evenly over fruit. Pour soda over cake mix, being sure to moisten as much of the mix as possible.

3. Bake for 35–40 minutes or until fruit is hot and bubbly.

NUTRITION FACTS

12 Servings

Amount Per Serving	
Calories	147.5
Total Fat	3.5 g
Saturated Fat	1.5 g
Polyunsaturated Fat	0 g
Monounsaturated Fat	0 g
Cholesterol	0 mg
Sodium	282 mg
Potassium	83 mg
Total Carbohydrate	36 g
Dietary Fiber	2 g
Sugars	4 g
Protein	1.5 g

Angel Berry Cake

Serves 16

INGREDIENTS:

½ of a ready-made angel food cake

2 cups low fat milk

2 boxes sugar-free vanilla pudding mix

1 quart reduced-fat strawberry ice cream, softened

1 box sugar-free strawberry Jell-O mix

1 ½ cups hot water

1 (10-ounce) bag frozen berries

DIRECTIONS:

1. Slice cake and arrange slices in bottom of 9 x 13 inch baking dish sprayed with light cooking spray.

2. Whisk together milk and pudding mix until pudding forms. Blend in ice cream and pour over angel food cake.

3. Mix together Jello-O and water. Stir in strawberries. Stir mixture until it begins to thicken. Pour over pudding. Refrigerate overnight.

NUTRITION FACTS

16 Servings

Amount Per Serving	
Calories	117.5
Total Fat	2.5 g
Saturated Fat	0 g
Polyunsaturated Fat	0 g
Monounsaturated Fat	0 g
Cholesterol	1.5 mg
Sodium	238 mg
Potassium	46 mg
Total Carbohydrate	28 g
Dietary Fiber	2.5 g
Sugars	5.5 g
Protein	4 g

Festive Fruit Cake

Serves 16

INGREDIENTS:

- 2 cups sugar blend
- 2 cups all-purpose flour
- 2 teaspoons baking soda
- 2 eggs or liquid egg substitute
- ½ teaspoon vanilla extract
- 1 (16-ounce) can no-sugar-added fruit cocktail

DIRECTIONS:

1. Preheat oven to 350 degrees F. Spray a 9 x 13 inch baking dish with light cooking spray.
2. Combine all ingredients in a large mixing bowl, and pour into the baking dish. Bake for 30–40 minutes or until cake is firm.

NUTRITION FACTS

16 Servings

Amount Per Serving	
Calories	189.5
Total Fat	0.5 g
Saturated Fat	0 g
Polyunsaturated Fat	0 g
Monounsaturated Fat	0 g
Cholesterol	23.5 mg
Sodium	166 mg
Potassium	29 mg
Total Carbohydrate	38 g
Dietary Fiber	0.5 g
Sugars	26.5 g
Protein	2.5 g

Sundae Toppings Pie

Serves 12

INGREDIENTS:

1 large box sugar-free vanilla pudding mix

1 ½ cups skim milk

4 bananas, sliced

2 cups strawberries, sliced

1 large can crushed pineapple in its own juice, drained

1 (8-ounce) container sugar-free frozen whipped topping, thawed

1 graham cracker pie crust

DIRECTIONS:

1. Whisk together pudding mix and milk until pudding forms. Pour into crust and refrigerate for 1 hour.

2. Arrange banana slices on top of pudding.

3. In a large bowl, mix together whipped topping, strawberries, and pineapple. Spread evenly over bananas. Serve chilled.

NUTRITION FACTS

12 Servings

Amount Per Serving	
Total Fat	5.5 g
Saturated Fat	1.5 g
Polyunsaturated Fat	1.5 g
Monounsaturated Fat	2 g
Cholesterol	0.5 mg
Sodium	213.5 mg
Potassium	300 mg
Total Carbohydrate	34 g
Dietary Fiber	2.5 g
Sugars	20 g
Protein	2.5 g
Protein	0 g

Pineapple Tiramisu

Serves 14

INGREDIENTS:

1 (8-ounce) package fat-free cream cheese

1 (8-ounce) package cream cheese, softened

⅔ cup sugar blend, divided

2 teaspoons vanilla extract

1 (8-ounce) package frozen fat-free whipped topping, thawed

3 (3-ounce) packages ladyfingers

3 tablespoons cornstarch

1 (20-ounce) can crushed pineapple

DIRECTIONS:

1. In a large bowl, beat the cream cheeses, ⅓ cup sugar, and vanilla until smooth. Fold in whipped topping.

2. In a small saucepan, combine the remaining sugar, cornstarch, and pineapple. Bring to a boil over medium heat, stirring constantly.

3. Cook 1–2 minutes or until thickened. Set aside to cool.

4. Arrange half the ladyfingers on the bottom of a 9 x 13 inch pan. Spread half the cream cheese mixture on top. Top with half the cooled pineapple. Make another layer of ladyfingers, cream cheese mixture, and pineapple. Cover with plastic wrap and refrigerate for at least 4 hours.

NUTRITION FACTS

14 Servings

Amount Per Serving	
Calories	252
Total Fat	7 g
Saturated Fat	4 g
Polyunsaturated Fat	0.5 g
Monounsaturated Fat	1 g
Cholesterol	89.5 mg
Sodium	205.5 mg
Potassium	80.5 mg
Total Carbohydrate	36.5 g
Dietary Fiber	0.5 g
Sugars	18.5 g
Protein	6 g

Family Favorite Pecan Pie

Serves 8

INGREDIENTS:

1 refrigerated pie crust

3 eggs or liquid egg substitute

5 teaspoons sugar blend

1 cup sugar-free breakfast syrup

1 teaspoon vanilla extract

⅓ cup butter, melted

1 cup pecan halves

DIRECTIONS:

1. Preheat oven to 350 degrees F. Lay pie crust in a 9-inch pie plate.

2. In a large bowl, mix together eggs and sugar blend. Stir in syrup, vanilla, and melted butter. Stir in pecans. Pour the mixture into the pie crust.

3. Bake 40–50 minutes or until pie begins to brown. Cool before serving.

NUTRITION FACTS

8 Servings

Amount Per Serving	
Calories	311.5
Total Fat	25 g
Saturated Fat	8.5 g
Polyunsaturated Fat	4 g
Monounsaturated Fat	11 g
Cholesterol	90.5 mg
Sodium	200 mg
Potassium	84.5 mg
Total Carbohydrate	20.5 g
Dietary Fiber	1.5 g
Sugars	3 g
Protein	3.5 g

Crustless Pumpkin Pie

Serves 8

INGREDIENTS:

1 (15-ounce) can solid-pack pumpkin

1 (12-ounce) can fat-free evaporated milk

1 cup egg substitute

¾ cup sugar blend

1 ½ teaspoons pumpkin pie spice

⅛ teaspoon salt

DIRECTIONS:

1. Preheat oven to 325 degrees F. In a large bowl, beat all ingredients together until well blended. Pour into a greased 9-inch pie plate.

2. Bake for 50 minutes or until a knife inserted near the center comes out clean.

NUTRITION FACTS

8 Servings

Amount Per Serving	
Calories	165
Total Fat	0.5 g
Saturated Fat	0 g
Polyunsaturated Fat	0 g
Monounsaturated Fat	0 g
Cholesterol	2 mg
Sodium	154 mg
Potassium	207.5 mg
Total Carbohydrate	29 g
Dietary Fiber	2.5 g
Sugars	25.5 g
Protein	8 g

Chocolate Raspberry Trifle

Serves 14

INGREDIENTS:

1 box sugar-free Devil's food cake mix,
   prepared, baked, and cut into chunks

1 package sugar-free, fat-free instant chocolate
   pudding mix, prepared

1 (12-ounce) package frozen raspberries, thawed

2 cups fat-free frozen whipped topping, thawed

DIRECTIONS:

1. In a large glass bowl, layer the cake,
   pudding, and raspberries. Top with
   whipped topping.

NUTRITION FACTS

14 Servings

Amount Per Serving	
Calories	230.5
Total Fat	13 g
Saturated Fat	3.5 g
Polyunsaturated Fat	2.5 g
Monounsaturated Fat	5 g
Cholesterol	40 mg
Sodium	251.5 mg
Potassium	60 mg
Total Carbohydrate	32.5 g
Dietary Fiber	3 g
Sugars	1.5 g
Protein	3.5 g

Chewy Coconut Squares

Serves 24

INGREDIENTS:

1 (12-ounce) bag shredded coconut

3 cups sugar blend

2 (12-ounce) cans non-fat or low-fat evaporated milk

1 ½ cups fat-free powdered milk

DIRECTIONS:

1. Spray a baking sheet with light cooking spray.
2. Combine all ingredients in a large saucepan, and cook over medium-low heat. Stir constantly for 20–30 minutes until mixture thickens.
3. Pour mixture onto baking sheet and spread to even thickness. Allow to cool before cutting into squares and serving.

NUTRITION FACTS

24 Servings

Amount Per Serving	
Calories	192.5
Total Fat	2.5 g
Saturated Fat	0 g
Polyunsaturated Fat	0 g
Monounsaturated Fat	0 g
Cholesterol	0.5 mg
Sodium	33.5 mg
Potassium	53 mg
Total Carbohydrate	33 g
Dietary Fiber	0.5 g
Sugars	26 g
Protein	4.5 g

Coconut Berry Macaroons

Serves 10

INGREDIENTS:

1 ¼ cup shredded coconut

½ cup sugar blend

Pinch of salt

2 egg whites

¼ cup non-fat strawberry Greek yogurt

2 teaspoons vanilla extract

½ cup diced strawberries

DIRECTIONS:

1. Preheat oven to 325 degrees F.

2. In a medium-sized bowl, mix together dry ingredients, then add in wet ingredients (except strawberries), and mix until well combined.

3. Stir in strawberries.

4. Drop dough onto a greased baking sheet and flatten dough into small discs using the back of a spoon to press down. Leave at least an inch between cookies.

5. Bake 25–35 minutes, or until lightly browned.

NUTRITION FACTS

10 Servings

Amount Per Serving	
Calories	311.5
Total Fat	18g
Saturated Fat	0 g
Polyunsaturated Fat	0 g
Monounsaturated Fat	0 g
Cholesterol	0 mg
Sodium	137 mg
Potassium	15 mg
Total Carbohydrate	36 g
Dietary Fiber	4 g
Sugars	10.5 g
Protein	5 g

Orange Cherry Cookies

Serves 12

INGREDIENTS:

1 ½ cups all-purpose flour

¾ cup whole-wheat flour

¼ cup sugar

2 teaspoons baking powder

¼ teaspoon salt

½ cup reduced-sugar orange juice

¼ cup vegetable oil

1 teaspoon orange rind, grated

1 egg, beaten or liquid egg substitute

¾ cup dried cherries, chopped

½ cup walnuts, chopped

DIRECTIONS:

1. Preheat oven to 375 degrees F.
2. In a medium-sized bowl, mix together flours, sugar, baking powder, and salt until combined. Add orange juice, oil, orange rind, and egg. Fold in cherries and walnuts.
3. Drop teaspoonfuls of dough onto an ungreased baking sheet, leaving 1 inch between them. Bake for 10–12 minutes, or until lightly browned.

NUTRITION FACTS

12 Servings

Amount Per Serving	
Calories	203
Total Fat	8.5 g
Saturated Fat	4 g
Polyunsaturated Fat	2.5 g
Monounsaturated Fat	0.5 g
Cholesterol	15.5 mg
Sodium	137.5 mg
Potassium	92 mg
Total Carbohydrate	28.5 g
Dietary Fiber	2 g
Sugars	8.5 g
Protein	4 g

Chocolate Chip Graham Sandwiches

Serves 21

INGREDIENTS:

1 package sugar-free instant vanilla pudding mix, prepared

2 cups reduced-fat frozen whipped topping, thawed

¾ cup miniature semisweet chocolate chips

21 reduced-fat graham crackers, halved

DIRECTIONS:

1. Mix together pudding, whipped topping, and chocolate chips.

2. Top half of the graham crackers with about 3 tablespoons of filling, and place the other graham cracker halves on top.

3. Freeze for 1 hour or until firm, then wrap individually in plastic wrap and freeze.

NUTRITION FACTS

21 Servings

Amount Per Serving	
Calories	136
Total Fat	4.5 g
Saturated Fat	2 g
Polyunsaturated Fat	0.5 g
Monounsaturated Fat	0 g
Cholesterol	3 mg
Sodium	285.5 mg
Potassium	28.5 mg
Total Carbohydrate	23.5 g
Dietary Fiber	1 g
Sugars	10 g
Protein	1.5 g

Oatmeal Raisin Cookies

Serves 15

INGREDIENTS:

½ cup butter, softened

½ cup applesauce

¼ cup sugar blend

¾ cup brown sugar blend

1 box sugar-free instant vanilla pudding mix

2 eggs or liquid egg substitute

1 ¼ cup all-purpose flour

1 teaspoon baking soda

3 ½ cups quick-cooking rolled oats

1 cup raisins, soaked in water to soften

DIRECTIONS:

1. Preheat oven to 375 degrees F. In a large mixing bowl, combine butter, applesauce, sugars, and pudding mix until smooth. Beat in eggs.

2. In a small bowl, mix flour with baking soda. Gradually add flour mixture to wet mixture.

3. Stir in oats and raisins. Drop teaspoonfuls of dough onto ungreased baking sheet about 2 inches apart.

4. Bake for 10–12 minutes.

NUTRITION FACTS

15 Servings

Amount Per Serving	
Calories	239.5
Total Fat	8 g
Saturated Fat	4 g
Polyunsaturated Fat	1 g
Monounsaturated Fat	2.5 g
Cholesterol	41.5 mg
Sodium	253 mg
Potassium	115.5 mg
Total Carbohydrate	40 g
Dietary Fiber	2.5 g
Sugars	13.5 g
Protein	4.5 g

Applesauce Raisin Loaf

Serves 10-12

INGREDIENTS:

2 cups all-purpose flour

1 tablespoon baking powder

½ teaspoon baking soda

½ teaspoon salt

8 packets sugar substitute

¼ teaspoon cinnamon

¼ teaspoon nutmeg

1 cup raisins

1 egg, beaten or liquid egg substitute

1 cup no-sugar-added applesauce

¼ cup vegetable oil

DIRECTIONS:

1. Preheat oven to 350 degrees F.

2. Combine dry ingredients in a large bowl. Stir in raisins. Make a well in center of dry mixture.

3. Whisk together egg, applesauce, and oil, and pour into well. Mix wet and dry ingredients, but be careful not to over mix.

4. Pour into a loaf pan that has been greased with light cooking spray and dusted with flour.

5. Bake 40–45 minutes or until a toothpick inserted in the center comes out clean. Allow to cool before slicing and serving.

NUTRITION FACTS

12 Servings

Amount Per Serving	
Calories	157.5
Total Fat	5 g
Saturated Fat	3.5 g
Polyunsaturated Fat	0 g
Monounsaturated Fat	0 g
Cholesterol	15.5 mg
Sodium	104.5 mg
Potassium	138.5 mg
Total Carbohydrate	26.5 g
Dietary Fiber	1.5 g
Sugars	9 g
Protein	3 g

Fresh Baked Zucchini Bread

Serves 10–12

INGREDIENTS:

⅓ cup brown sugar blend

½ cup unsweetened applesauce

¼ cup canola oil

4 egg whites

1 teaspoon vanilla

1 cup whole-wheat flour

1 cup old fashioned, rolled oats

2 teaspoons baking powder

1 teaspoon baking soda

½ teaspoon salt

1 teaspoon cinnamon

2 cups zucchini, shredded

DIRECTIONS:

1. Preheat oven to 350 degrees F. Lightly spray a loaf pan with light cooking spray and dust with flour.

2. In a large bowl, mix together the first 5 ingredients.

3. In a separate bowl, combine all dry ingredients. Stir in zucchini. Make a well in center of dry mixture and add wet mixture. Mix well.

4. Pour into loaf pan and bake for 50–60 minutes.

NUTRITION FACTS

12 Servings

Amount Per Serving	
Calories	123
Total Fat	5 g
Saturated Fat	0.5 g
Polyunsaturated Fat	1.5 g
Monounsaturated Fat	3 g
Cholesterol	0 mg
Sodium	117.5 mg
Potassium	123.5 mg
Total Carbohydrate	17.5 g
Dietary Fiber	1.5 g
Sugars	4.5 g
Protein	3.5 g

Cinnamon French Toast

Serves 4

INGREDIENTS:

3 eggs

¼ cup low-fat milk

½ teaspoon vanilla extract

½ teaspoon cinnamon

8 slices whole-wheat bread

DIRECTIONS:

1. Whisk together eggs and milk. Add vanilla and cinnamon to egg mixture.
2. Drench bread slices in egg mixture and place bread on a griddle or large frying pan.
3. Cook in batches until slices are golden brown on both sides.

NUTRITION FACTS

4 Servings

Amount Per Serving	
Calories	185
Total Fat	6 g
Saturated Fat	1.5 g
Polyunsaturated Fat	1 g
Monounsaturated Fat	1.5 g
Cholesterol	141.5 mg
Sodium	281 mg
Potassium	76.5 mg
Total Carbohydrates	23 g
Dietary Fiber	4 g
Sugars	3 g
Protein	13 g

Peanut Butter and Banana Pudding

Serves 12

INGREDIENTS:

1 box sugar-free instant vanilla pudding mix

2 cups fat-free milk

⅓ cup no-added-sugar creamy peanut butter

1 (8-ounce) container fat-free sour cream

3–4 bananas, sliced

1 cup chocolate chips

DIRECTIONS:

1. Whisk together pudding mix and milk until pudding forms. Add peanut butter and sour cream, and mix until well combined. Chill in refrigerator for 1 hour.

2. Portion pudding into dessert glasses. Top with bananas and chocolate chips.

NUTRITION FACTS

12 Servings

Amount Per Serving	
Calories	222.5
Total Fat	9 g
Saturated Fat	4 g
Polyunsaturated Fat	0 g
Monounsaturated Fat	0 g
Cholesterol	1 mg
Sodium	361 mg
Potassium	187 mg
Total Carbohydrate	31 g
Dietary Fiber	1.5 g
Sugars	18.5 g
Protein	4 g

Warm Harvest Pudding

Serves 6

INGREDIENTS:

½ cup egg substitute

2 cups pumpkin pie filling

¼ cup sugar blend

1 tablespoon flour

¼ teaspoon salt

¼ teaspoon cinnamon

¼ teaspoon nutmeg

1 cup fat-free milk

DIRECTIONS:

1. Preheat the oven to 350 degrees F. Mix together all ingredients until well combined. Pour into a square baking dish coated with light cooking spray.

2. Bake for 25–35 minutes. Serve warm.

NUTRITION FACTS

6 Servings

Amount Per Serving	
Calories	136
Total Fat	0.5 g
Saturated Fat	0 g
Polyunsaturated Fat	0 g
Monounsaturated Fat	0 g
Cholesterol	1 mg
Sodium	275.5 mg
Potassium	96.5 mg
Total Carbohydrate	28 g
Dietary Fiber	3 g
Sugars	23.5 g
Protein	4.5 g

Grandma's Bread Pudding

Serves 6

INGREDIENTS:

2 slices wheat bread, cubed

½ cup raisins

2 cups fat-free milk

2 large eggs, slightly beaten, or ½ cup liquid egg substitute

2 tablespoons sugar blend

1 teaspoon ground cinnamon

1 teaspoon pure vanilla extract

Pinch salt

DIRECTIONS:

1. Preheat the oven to 350 degrees F. Prepare a 9 x 9 inch baking dish with light cooking spray.

2. Add bread cubes and raisins to the baking dish to cover the bottom.

3. In a medium sized bowl, mix together remaining ingredients. Pour over bread. Stir gently until blended.

4. Bake 40–55 minutes, or until a knife inserted in the center comes out clean.

NUTRITION FACTS

6 Servings

Amount Per Serving	
Calories	107
Total Fat	0.5 g
Saturated Fat	0 g
Polyunsaturated Fat	0 g
Monounsaturated Fat	0 g
Cholesterol	1.5 mg
Sodium	117 mg
Potassium	259 mg
Total Carbohydrate	20.5 g
Dietary Fiber	0.5 g
Sugars	14 g
Protein	6 g

Chocolate Mousse Cups

Serves 6

INGREDIENTS:

- 1 box sugar-free chocolate pudding mix
- 1 ½ cups low-fat milk
- 1 ½ cups fat-free frozen whipped topping, thawed
- ¾ cup frozen raspberries, thawed

DIRECTIONS:

1. Whisk together pudding mix and milk until pudding forms. Cover with plastic wrap and chill in refrigerator for 1 hour.
2. Fold in whipped topping. Portion into 6 cupcake tin liners, and serve with raspberries as a topping.

NUTRITION FACTS

6 Servings

Amount Per Serving	
Calories	104
Total Fat	2.5 g
Saturated Fat	2.5 g
Polyunsaturated Fat	0 g
Monounsaturated Fat	0 g
Cholesterol	3 mg
Sodium	330 mg
Potassium	118 mg
Total Carbohydrate	15 g
Dietary Fiber	1 g
Sugars	8 g
Protein	2.5 g

Grapefruit and Berry Medley

Serves 6

INGREDIENTS:

2 pink grapefruits, peeled and sectioned

2 oranges, peeled and sectioned

1 cup strawberries, quartered

1 cup blueberries

1 lime or ¼ cup lime juice

Fresh mint sprigs

DIRECTIONS:

1. In a large bowl, add grapefruit, oranges, strawberries, and blueberries.

2. Squeeze or pour lime juice into bowl and stir to coat. Cover and chill, or serve immediately with mint as garnish.

NUTRITION FACTS

6 Servings

Amount Per Serving	
Calories	77
Total Fat	0 g
Saturated Fat	0 g
Polyunsaturated Fat	0 g
Monounsaturated Fat	0 g
Cholesterol	0 mg
Sodium	2 mg
Potassium	290 mg
Total Carbohydrate	19.5 g
Dietary Fiber	3.5 g
Sugars	15.5 g
Protein	1.5 g

Blackberry Banana Smoothie

Serves 4

INGREDIENTS:

2 cups frozen blackberries

½ banana

1 cup low-fat vanilla yogurt, softened

1 ½ cups low-fat or almond milk

DIRECTIONS:

1. Combine all ingredients in a blender and process until smooth. Serve immediately.

NUTRITION FACTS

4 Servings

Amount Per Serving	
Calories	149.5
Total Fat	3 g
Saturated Fat	1.5 g
Polyunsaturated Fat	0 g
Monounsaturated Fat	0.5 g
Cholesterol	9.5 mg
Sodium	61 mg
Potassium	371 mg
Total Carbohydrate	30 g
Dietary Fiber	4 g
Sugars	23.5 g
Protein	6 g

Perfect Piña Colada Smoothie

Serves 3

INGREDIENTS:

1 banana

½ cup light coconut milk

2 cups canned pineapple chunks

1 cup crushed ice

DIRECTIONS:

1. Combine all ingredients in a blender and process until smooth. Serve immediately.

NUTRITION FACTS

3 Servings

Amount Per Serving	
Calories	136.0
Total Fat	0.9 g
Saturated Fat	0.7 g
Polyunsaturated Fat	0.0 g
Monounsaturated Fat	0.0 g
Cholesterol	0.0 mg
Sodium	0.5 mg
Potassium	347.5 mg
Total Carbohydrate	30.7 g
Dietary Fiber	2.5 g
Sugars	24.8 g
Protein	1.1 g

Choco-Peanut Butter Smoothie

Serves 2

INGREDIENTS:

2 cups almond milk, unsweetened

1 cup low-fat chocolate milk

Sugar substitute equivalent of 1 tablespoon sugar

2 tablespoons unsweetened cocoa powder

2 tablespoons no-sugar-added creamy
     peanut butter

DIRECTIONS:

1. Process all ingredients in a blender until smooth. Serve immediately.

NUTRITION FACTS

2 Servings

Amount Per Serving	
Calories	221
Total Fat	12.5 g
Saturated Fat	2.5 g
Polyunsaturated Fat	2.5 g
Monounsaturated Fat	4.5 g
Cholesterol	4 mg
Sodium	310 mg
Potassium	465 mg
Total Carbohydrate	21 g
Dietary Fiber	4.5 g
Sugars	13 g
Protein	9.5 g

Strawberries with Fluffy Chocolate Dip

Serves 10

INGREDIENTS:

- 1 package sugar-free instant chocolate pudding mix, prepared
- 1 ¾ cups reduced-fat frozen whipped topping, thawed
- 2 quarts strawberries

DIRECTIONS:

1. Combine the pudding and the whipped topping. Serve with strawberries for dipping.

NUTRITION FACTS

10 Servings

Amount Per Serving	
Calories	112.5
Total Fat	2 g
Saturated Fat	1.5 g
Polyunsaturated Fat	0 g
Monounsaturated Fat	0 g
Cholesterol	0 mg
Sodium	488 mg
Potassium	202 mg
Total Carbohydrate	18 g
Dietary Fiber	3 g
Sugars	9 g
Protein	0.5 g

Jiggly Apple Squares

Serves 8

INGREDIENTS:

3 cups no-sugar-added apple juice

4 envelopes unflavored gelatin

1 ½ cups apple, peeled and diced

DIRECTIONS:

1. In a small saucepan, bring apple juice to a boil. Add gelatin to saucepan and stir until dissolved. Pour into a shallow pan.

2. Allow gelatin to set for 15 minutes in refrigerator. Mix in apples. Refrigerate for 3–4 more hours before cutting into squares and serving.

NUTRITION FACTS

8 Servings

Amount Per Serving	
Calories	58.5
Total Fat	0 g
Saturated Fat	0 g
Polyunsaturated Fat	0 g
Monounsaturated Fat	0 g
Cholesterol	0 mg
Sodium	3 mg
Potassium	136 mg
Total Carbohydrate	14.1 g
Dietary Fiber	0.5 g
Sugars	2.5 g
Protein	0.5 g

Amazing Applesauce

Serves 6

INGREDIENTS:

- 4 large apples, peeled and cut into chunks
- 3 tablespoons sugar blend
- 2 tablespoons lemon juice
- ½ teaspoon cinnamon

DIRECTIONS:

1. Combine all ingredients in a medium saucepan.
2. Cover and cook over low heat until apples are soft, about 15 minutes.
3. Stir with a spoon to break up apples, and serve.

NUTRITION FACTS

6 Servings

Amount Per Serving	
Calories	86.5
Total Fat	0 g
Saturated Fat	0 g
Polyunsaturated Fat	0 g
Monounsaturated Fat	0 g
Cholesterol	0 mg
Sodium	1 mg
Potassium	156.5 mg
Total Carbohydrate	23 g
Dietary Fiber	3.5 g
Sugars	18 g
Protein	0.5 g

Summer Berries with Maple Cream

Serves 4

INGREDIENTS:

> ¾ cup fat-free sour cream
>
> ¼ cup maple syrup
>
> 2 ½ cups mixed berries

DIRECTIONS:

1. Stir together sour cream and maple syrup.
2. Divide berries among 4 dishes and top with the maple cream.

NUTRITION FACTS

4 Servings

Amount Per Serving	
Calories	125
Total Fat	0 g
Saturated Fat	0 g
Polyunsaturated Fat	0 g
Monounsaturated Fat	0 g
Cholesterol	0 mg
Sodium	39.5 mg
Potassium	146.5 mg
Total Carbohydrate	28.5 g
Dietary Fiber	3 g
Sugars	21 g
Protein	2 g

Chocolate Fizzy Float

Serves 6

INGREDIENTS:

- 1 ½ cups no-sugar-added, reduced-fat chocolate ice cream
- 3 ½ cups plain seltzer

DIRECTIONS:

1. Divide the ice cream into six tall glasses, and pour the seltzer over the top.

Amount Per Serving	
Calories	65
Total Fat	5 g
Saturated Fat	0 g
Polyunsaturated Fat	0 g
Monounsaturated Fat	0 g
Cholesterol	12.5 mg
Sodium	25 mg
Potassium	0 mg
Total Carbohydrate	5 g
Dietary Fiber	1.5 g
Sugars	2 g
Protein	1 g

Root Beer Float

Serves 6

INGREDIENTS:

- 1 ½ cups no-sugar-added, reduced-fat vanilla ice cream
- 3 ½ cups diet root beer

DIRECTIONS:

1. Divide the ice cream into six tall glasses and pour the root beer over the top.

NUTRITION FACTS

6 Servings

Amount Per Serving	
Calories	65
Total Fat	4.5 g
Saturated Fat	0 g
Polyunsaturated Fat	0 g
Monounsaturated Fat	0 g
Cholesterol	12.5 mg
Sodium	112.5 mg
Potassium	0 mg
Total Carbohydrate	5 g
Dietary Fiber	1.5 g
Sugars	2 g
Protein	1 g

Frozen Cookies 'n Cream Cake

Serves 9

INGREDIENTS:

- 1 (6 ½-ounce) package sugar-free chocolate sandwich cookies, crushed
- ⅓ cup walnuts, chopped
- 3 tablespoons butter, melted
- 1 quart no-sugar-added vanilla ice cream, softened

DIRECTIONS:

1. Combine cookies, nuts, and butter in a small bowl. Set aside 1 cup of this mixture.
2. Press the remaining mixture firmly into the bottom of an 8-inch square pan.
3. Freeze for 10 minutes.
4. Spread the ice cream over the crust in the pan, and sprinkle with the reserved crumb mixture.
5. Cover with plastic wrap and freeze until firm, about 8 hours.

NUTRITION FACTS

9 Servings

Amount Per Serving	
Calories	236.8
Total Fat	15.3 g
Saturated Fat	6.2 g
Polyunsaturated Fat	2.8 g
Monounsaturated Fat	4.1 g
Cholesterol	26.2 mg
Sodium	106.5 mg
Potassium	149.0 mg
Total Carbohydrate	25.6 g
Dietary Fiber	0.9 g
Sugars	4.0 g
Protein	3.9 g

Creamy Lime Salad with Raspberries

Serves 8

INGREDIENTS:

1 box sugar-free lime Jello-O mix

1 cup boiling water

1 pint lime sherbet, softened

1 container fat-free frozen whipped topping, thawed

2 cups frozen raspberries, thawed

DIRECTIONS:

1. In a large bowl, dissolve Jello-O powder in boiling water. Stir in sherbet until fully combined. Add in whipped topping and beat with an electric mixer on Low until well blended. Fold in frozen berries.

2. Pour into a lightly greased Bundt cake pan or Jello-O mold.

3. Refrigerate 4–6 hours or until firm. Remove from mold and serve.

NUTRITION FACTS

8 Servings

Amount Per Serving	
Calories	132.5
Total Fat	3 g
Saturated Fat	3 g
Polyunsaturated Fat	0 g
Monounsaturated Fat	0 g
Cholesterol	5 mg
Sodium	47.5 mg
Potassium	53 mg
Total Carbohydrate	23 g
Dietary Fiber	2.5 g
Sugars	16.5 g
Protein	1.5 g

Frozen Strawberry Shortcake

Serves 9

INGREDIENTS:

1 package sugar-free vanilla sandwich cookies, crushed

3 tablespoons butter, melted

1 (16-ounce) package frozen strawberries, thawed

1 quart no-sugar-added vanilla ice cream, softened

DIRECTIONS:

1. Combine cookies and butter in a small bowl. Press the mixture firmly into the bottom of an 8-inch square pan. Freeze for 10 minutes.

2. Mix the strawberries and ice cream together in a bowl, and then spread over the crust.

3. Cover with plastic wrap and freeze until firm, about 8 hours.

NUTRITION FACTS

9 Servings

Amount Per Serving	
Calories	205.5
Total Fat	11 g
Saturated Fat	4.5 g
Polyunsaturated Fat	0.5 g
Monounsaturated Fat	1.5 g
Cholesterol	18 mg
Sodium	144 mg
Potassium	129.5 mg
Total Carbohydrate	28.5 g
Dietary Fiber	1 g
Sugars	4 g
Protein	2.5 g

Raspberry Almond Cake

Serves 2

INGREDIENTS:

- 4 tablespoons self-rising flour
- 3 tablespoons sugar blend
- 2 tablespoons liquid egg substitute
- 3 tablespoons skim milk
- 2 tablespoons vegetable oil
- ¼ teaspoon almond extract
- 1 handful fresh or frozen raspberries, thawed

DIRECTIONS:

1. Mix flour and sugar together in a mug. Add egg substitute, milk, oil, and extract and mix until fully combined. Stir in raspberries. Divide between two small mugs.

2. Microwave on high 1 minute, or until tops of mug cakes are dry.

NUTRITION FACTS

2 Servings

Amount Per Serving	
Calories	230.5
Total Fat	14 g
Saturated Fat	10 g
Polyunsaturated Fat	0 g
Monounsaturated Fat	0 g
Cholesterol	0.5 mg
Sodium	240.5 mg
Potassium	90.5 mg
Total Carbohydrate	32 g
Dietary Fiber	1 g
Sugars	30.5 g
Protein	4 g

Blueberry Lemon Cake

Serves 2

INGREDIENTS:

- 4 tablespoons self-rising flour
- 3 tablespoons sugar blend
- 2 tablespoons liquid egg substitute
- 3 tablespoons skim milk
- 1 tablespoons vegetable oil
- 1 tablespoon fresh lemon juice
- 1 handful fresh or frozen blueberries, thawed

DIRECTIONS:

1. Mix flour and sugar together in a mug. Add egg substitute, milk, oil, and lemon juice and mix until fully combined. Stir in blueberries. Divide between two small mugs.

2. Microwave on high 1 minute, or until top of mug cakes are dry.

NUTRITION FACTS

2 Servings

Amount Per Serving	
Calories	170.5
Total Fat	7 g
Saturated Fat	5 g
Polyunsaturated Fat	0 g
Monounsaturated Fat	0 g
Cholesterol	0.5 mg
Sodium	241 mg
Potassium	85 mg
Total Carbohydrate	32 g
Dietary Fiber	0.5 g
Sugars	31 g
Protein	4 g

No Bake Pineapple Pie

Serves 8

INGREDIENTS:

- 1 box sugar-free instant vanilla pudding mix
- 1 cup cold low-fat milk
- 1 (8-ounce) can crushed pineapple, drained
- 1 (8-ounce) container frozen light whipped topping, thawed
- 1 9-inch ready-made graham cracker crust

DIRECTIONS:

1. In a medium-sized mixing bowl, whisk together pudding mix and milk.
2. Fold in pineapple and whipped topping. Pour mixture into prepared crust. Chill for 3–4 hours and serve.

NUTRITION FACTS

8 Servings

Amount Per Serving	
Calories	183
Total Fat	7.5 g
Saturated Fat	2.5 g
Polyunsaturated Fat	2 g
Monounsaturated Fat	3 g
Cholesterol	0 mg
Sodium	342.5 mg
Potassium	60.5 mg
Total Carbohydrates	27.5 g
Dietary Fiber	0.5 g
Sugars	16 g
Protein	1.5 g

Berry Supreme Dump Cake

Serves 12

INGREDIENTS:

2 (12-ounce) bags frozen mixed berries

1 (18-ounce) box sugar-free yellow cake mix

1 can diet Sprite

DIRECTIONS:

1. Preheat oven to 350 degrees F. Spray a 9 x 13 inch dish with light cooking spray.

2. Cover bottom of cake pan with the frozen fruit. Sprinkle the cake mix over the fruit.

3. Pour soda over cake mix being careful to moisten as much of the mix as possible. Cover with foil.

4. Bake 20 minutes. Remove from oven, uncover, and coat top of dessert with cooking spray. Bake an additional 25–30 minutes.

NUTRITION FACTS

12 Servings

Amount Per Serving	
Calories	137.5
Total Fat	3.5 g
Saturated Fat	1.5 g
Polyunsaturated Fat	0 g
Monounsaturated Fat	0 g
Cholesterol	0 mg
Sodium	286 mg
Potassium	0 mg
Total Carbohydrates	33.5 g
Dietary Fiber	1.5 g
Sugars	3 g
Protein	1.5 g

Perfectly Easy Pumpkin Cake

Serves 12

INGREDIENTS:

- 2 (15-ounce) cans 100% pure pumpkin pie filling
- 1 box sugar-free yellow cake mix
- 1 can diet soda
- 1 teaspoon pumpkin pie spice
- 1 tablespoon sugar substitute

DIRECTIONS:

1. Preheat the oven to 350 degrees F. Grease a 9 x 13 inch baking dish with cooking spray.

2. Cover the bottom of the baking dish with pumpkin pie filling. Sprinkle the cake mix over the pumpkin pie filling. Pour soda over cake mix to moisten.

3. Sprinkle spice and sugar on top. Bake for 35–40 minutes or until the cake is hot and bubbly.

NUTRITION FACTS

12 Servings

Amount Per Serving	
Calories	152
Total Fat	4 g
Saturated Fat	1.5 g
Polyunsaturated Fat	0 g
Monounsaturated Fat	0 g
Cholesterol	0 mg
Sodium	286.5 mg
Potassium	1 mg
Total Carbohydrate	36 g
Dietary Fiber	4 g
Sugars	3.5 g
Protein	2.5 g

4-Ingredient Apple Cobbler

Serves 12

INGREDIENTS:

- 2 (21-ounce) cans no-sugar-added apple pie filling
- 1 box sugar-free vanilla cake mix
- ½ teaspoon cinnamon
- 1 can diet soda

DIRECTIONS:

1. Preheat oven to 350 degrees F. Grease a 9 x 13 inch baking dish with light cooking spray.
2. Spread pie filling to cover bottom of baking dish. Sprinkle cake mix over pie filling. Pour soda over mix to moisten. Do not mix.
3. Bake for 35–40 minutes or until the top of the cake begins to brown.

NUTRITION FACTS

12 Servings

Amount Per Serving	
Calories	166
Total Fat	5 g
Saturated Fat	1.5 g
Polyunsaturated Fat	0 g
Monounsaturated Fat	0 g
Cholesterol	0 mg
Sodium	284 mg
Potassium	0 mg
Total Carbohydrates	29 g
Dietary Fiber	0.5 g
Sugars	0 g
Protein	1 g

Caramel Apple Cake

Serves 12

INGREDIENTS:

2 cans no-sugar-added apple pie filling

1 box sugar-free yellow cake mix

1 can diet cream soda

½ cup chopped walnuts

⅓ cup caramel sauce

DIRECTIONS:

1. Preheat the oven to 350 degrees F. Grease a 9 x 13 inch baking dish with light cooking spray.

2. Pour pie filling into baking dish and spread evenly along bottom of dish. Sprinkle on cake mix. Pour soda over cake mix.

3. Sprinkle on walnuts. Drizzle with caramel sauce. Bake 35–40 minutes or until hot and bubbly.

NUTRITION FACTS

12 Servings

Amount Per Serving	
Calories	212
Total Fat	8 g
Saturated Fat	2 g
Polyunsaturated Fat	2.5 g
Monounsaturated Fat	0.5 g
Cholesterol	1 mg
Sodium	299 mg
Potassium	0.5 mg
Total Carbohydrates	36 g
Dietary Fiber	1 g
Sugars	5 g
Protein	1.5 g

Strawberry Angel Food Cake

Serves 12

INGREDIENTS:

- 1 (20-ounce) bag frozen strawberries, thawed or fresh strawberries
- 1 box sugar-free Angel Food cake mix
- 1 can diet lemon-lime soda
- 1 (8-ounce) container light frozen whipped topping

DIRECTIONS:

1. Preheat oven to 350 degrees F. Coat the bottom of a 9 x 13 inch baking dish with light cooking spray.
2. Cover bottom of dish with strawberries. Sprinkle on cake mix. Pour soda over cake mix.
3. Bake for 30–40 minutes.
4. Once the cake is cooled, serve with whipped topping.

NUTRITION FACTS

12 Servings

Amount Per Serving	
Calories	148.5
Total Fat	2 g
Saturated Fat	1.5 g
Polyunsaturated Fat	0 g
Monounsaturated Fat	0 g
Cholesterol	0.5 mg
Sodium	253 mg
Potassium	96.5 mg
Total Carbohydrate	30.5 g
Dietary Fiber	0.5 g
Sugars	22 g
Protein	3 g

Chocolate Parfait

Serves 2

INGREDIENTS:

- 1 box sugar-free chocolate pudding mix
- 1 cup low-fat milk
- 1 cup light frozen whipped topping
- ¼ cup tiny marshmallows

DIRECTIONS:

1. Prepare pudding by whisking together pudding mix and milk.
2. In two dessert glasses, add alternate layers of pudding and whipped topping until glass is full. Sprinkle on marshmallows and serve.

NUTRITION FACTS

2 Servings

Amount Per Serving	
Calories	222.5
Total Fat	6 g
Saturated Fat	5 g
Polyunsaturated Fat	0 g
Monounsaturated Fat	0.5 g
Cholesterol	8.5 mg
Sodium	92 mg
Potassium	38 mg
Total Carbohydrate	30.5 g
Dietary Fiber	0 g
Sugars	17.5 g
Protein	7 g

Lemon Raspberry Cream Pie

Serves 8

INGREDIENTS:

- 1 box sugar-free lemon Jell-O mix
- 1 (8-ounce) container light frozen whipped topping, thawed
- 8 ounces fat-free plain yogurt
- 1 reduced-fat ready-made graham cracker crust
- 1 cup fresh raspberries

DIRECTIONS:

1. In a large bowl, combine Jell-O mix, frozen whipped topping, and yogurt.
2. Pour into graham cracker crust and refrigerate until set. Top with fresh raspberries or serve raspberries on the side.

NUTRITION FACTS

8 Servings

Amount Per Serving	
Calories	232.5
Total Fat	10.5 g
Saturated Fat	4.5 g
Polyunsaturated Fat	2 g
Monounsaturated Fat	3.5 g
Cholesterol	0 mg
Sodium	212 mg
Potassium	50 mg
Total Carbohydrate	32.5 g
Dietary Fiber	2 g
Sugars	16 g
Protein	3 g

Applesauce Cake

Serves 2

INGREDIENTS:

- 4 tablespoons self-rising flour
- 3 tablespoons brown sugar blend
- ¼ teaspoon cinnamon
- 3 tablespoons unsweetened applesauce
- 2 tablespoons skim milk
- 2 tablespoons vegetable oil

DIRECTIONS:

1. In a small bowl, mix flour, brown sugar, and cinnamon.
2. Add the applesauce, milk, and oil and stir. Divide between two small mugs.
3. Microwave on high for 1 minute, or until tops of mug cakes are dry.

NUTRITION FACTS

2 Servings

Amount Per Serving	
Calories	208
Total Fat	14 g
Saturated Fat	10 g
Polyunsaturated Fat	0 g
Monounsaturated Fat	0 g
Cholesterol	0.5 mg
Sodium	207 mg
Potassium	61 mg
Total Carbohydrate	33 g
Dietary Fiber	1 g
Sugars	32 g
Protein	2 g

Raspberry Chocolate Cake

Serves 12

INGREDIENTS:

2 (12-ounce) bags frozen raspberries, thawed

1 box sugar-free chocolate cake mix

1 can diet soda or diet cherry soda

DIRECTIONS:

1. Preheat oven to 350 degrees F. Coat a 9 x 13 inch baking dish with light cooking spray.
2. Cover bottom of dish with raspberries. Sprinkle on cake mix. Pour soda over cake mix.
3. Bake for 30–40 minutes.

NUTRITION FACTS

12 Servings

Amount Per Serving	
Calories	134.5
Total Fat	3.5 g
Saturated Fat	1.5 g
Polyunsaturated Fat	0 g
Monounsaturated Fat	0 g
Cholesterol	0 mg
Sodium	254 mg
Potassium	44 mg
Total Carbohydrates	32.5 g
Dietary Fiber	3 g
Sugars	1.5 g
Protein	2.5 g

Cherry Supreme Corn Bread

Serves 18

INGREDIENTS:

2 (21-ounce) cans no-sugar-added cherry pie
   filling

1 (8.5-ounce) box corn bread or corn muffin mix

½ box sugar-free yellow cake mix

1 can lemon-lime soda

DIRECTIONS:

1. Preheat oven to 350 degrees F. Grease
    a 9 x 13 inch baking dish with light
    cooking spray.

2. Spread pie filling to cover bottom of baking
    dish. Sprinkle both mixes over pie filling.
    Pour the soda over mixes to moisten.
    Do not mix.

3. Bake for 35–40 minutes or until top of cake
    begins to brown.

NUTRITION FACTS

18 Servings

Amount Per Serving	
Calories	164
Total Fat	4 g
Saturated Fat	1.5 g
Polyunsaturated Fat	0 g
Monounsaturated Fat	0 g
Cholesterol	11.5 mg
Sodium	288.5 mg
Potassium	71 mg
Total Carbohydrate	34.5 g
Dietary Fiber	0.5 g
Sugars	4.5 g
Protein	1.5 g

Choco-Banana Puree

Serves 4

INGREDIENTS:

3 bananas, peeled and frozen

2 tablespoons sugar-free chocolate syrup

½ cup frozen light whipped topping

DIRECTIONS:

1. Process bananas and chocolate syrup together in a food processor until smooth.
2. Divide puree into four small dessert glasses. Top with whipped topping.

NUTRITION FACTS

4 Servings

Amount Per Serving	
Calories	144
Total Fat	2.5 g
Saturated Fat	2 g
Polyunsaturated Fat	0 g
Monounsaturated Fat	0 g
Cholesterol	0 mg
Sodium	5 mg
Potassium	334.5 mg
Total Carbohydrate	32 g
Dietary Fiber	2.5 g
Sugars	18 g
Protein	1 g

Strawberry Cream Pie

Serves 8

INGREDIENTS:

1 box sugar-free strawberry Jell-O mix

1 (8-ounce) container light frozen whipped
topping, thawed

8 ounces fat-free strawberry yogurt

1 reduced-fat ready-made graham cracker crust

1 cup fresh strawberries, sliced

DIRECTIONS:

1. In a large bowl, combine Jell-O mix,
frozen whipped topping, and yogurt.

2. Pour into graham cracker crust and
refrigerate until set. Serve with sliced
strawberries as topping.

NUTRITION FACTS

8 Servings

Amount Per Serving	
Calories	199.5
Total Fat	9 g
Saturated Fat	3 g
Polyunsaturated Fat	2 g
Monounsaturated Fat	3.5 g
Cholesterol	1.5 mg
Sodium	211 mg
Potassium	102 mg
Total Carbohydrates	25.5 g
Dietary Fiber	1 g
Sugars	15.5 g
Protein	2.5 g

Dump and Chill Raspberry Cheesecake

Serves 8

INGREDIENTS:

1 (8-ounce) package reduced-fat cream cheese

¼ cup milk

½ teaspoon vanilla extract

⅓ cup sugar substitute, such as Stevia

1 ready-made graham cracker piecrust

3 cups fresh or frozen raspberries, thawed

DIRECTIONS:

1. In a medium sized bowl, mix together the first 4 ingredients until well blended. Empty into piecrust.
2. Top with raspberries and chill in the refrigerator before serving.

NUTRITION FACTS

8 Servings

Amount Per Serving	
Calories	226.5
Total Fat	12 g
Saturated Fat	5 g
Polyunsaturated Fat	2 g
Monounsaturated Fat	4.5 g
Cholesterol	17.5 mg
Sodium	243 mg
Potassium	157.5 mg
Total Carbohydrates	25 g
Dietary Fiber	3.5 g
Sugars	10.5 g
Protein	5 g

Microwave Rice Pudding

Serves 6

INGREDIENTS:

1 box sugar-free vanilla pudding mix
2 cups nonfat evaporated milk
½ cup white or brown rice, cooked
Pinch cinnamon

DIRECTIONS:

1. Mix together pudding mix, milk, and rice in a microwave-safe bowl.

2. Microwave for 12–15 minutes, stirring every few minutes, until mixture thickens into a pudding. Sprinkle with cinnamon and serve.

NUTRITION FACTS

6 Servings

Amount Per Serving	
Calories	121.5
Total Fat	0 g
Saturated Fat	0 g
Polyunsaturated Fat	0 g
Monounsaturated Fat	0 g
Cholesterol	0 mg
Sodium	665 mg
Potassium	243 mg
Total Carbohydrates	24.5 g
Dietary Fiber	0 g
Sugars	8.5 g
Protein	4.5 g

30-Second Brownies

Serves 1

INGREDIENTS:

- 1 tablespoon self-rising flour
- 1 tablespoon cocoa powder
- 1 tablespoon brown sugar
- 1 tablespoon water
- 1 tablespoon canola oil

DIRECTIONS:

1. Mix all ingredients together in a small bowl or a mug and heat in microwave for 30 seconds.

NUTRITION FACTS

1 Servings

Amount Per Serving	
Calories	197
Total Fat	14.5 g
Saturated Fat	1.5 g
Polyunsaturated Fat	4 g
Monounsaturated Fat	8.5 g
Cholesterol	0 mg
Sodium	1.5 mg
Potassium	90.5 mg
Total Carbohydrates	17 g
Dietary Fiber	2 g
Sugars	8 g
Protein	2 g

Cinnamon Apples

Serves 2

INGREDIENTS:

2 medium cooking apples, peeled and sliced
½-inch thick

1 tablespoon butter

2 tablespoons sugar substitute or sugar blend

1 teaspoon ground cinnamon

Dash nutmeg

Dash salt

DIRECTIONS:

1. Heat butter in a skillet over medium heat. Add apples to the skillet.

2. Sprinkle apples with cinnamon, nutmeg, salt, and half of the sugar substitute.

3. Reduce heat to low and cook apples for 5 minutes. Sprinkle on remaining sugar substitute and cook until apples are soft. Serve warm.

NUTRITION FACTS

2 Servings

Amount Per Serving	
Calories	123
Total Fat	6 g
Saturated Fat	3.5 g
Polyunsaturated Fat	0.5 g
Monounsaturated Fat	1.5 g
Cholesterol	15.5 mg
Sodium	118.5 mg
Potassium	149.5 mg
Total Carbohydrates	19 g
Dietary Fiber	3.5 g
Sugars	14.5 g
Protein	0.5 g

Orange Soda Cupcakes

Serves 24

INGREDIENTS:

1 box sugar-free yellow cake mix

1 can diet orange soda

DIRECTIONS:

1. Preheat oven to 350 degrees F.
2. Blend ingredients together with an electric mixer in a large bowl.
3. Pour into cupcake lined muffin tins. Bake for 15–18 minutes, or until a toothpick comes out clean after inserted in the middle of the cupcake.

NUTRITION FACTS

24 Servings

Amount Per Serving	
Calories	60
Total Fat	2 g
Saturated Fat	1 g
Polyunsaturated Fat	0 g
Monounsaturated Fat	0 g
Cholesterol	0 mg
Sodium	142 mg
Potassium	0 mg
Total Carbohydrates	14.5 g
Dietary Fiber	0.5 g
Sugars	0 g
Protein	0.5 g

Using This Food Journal

Many people can benefit from keeping a food journal, but it's especially important to keep one when you have diabetes. Use the following food journal pages to get in the habit of writing down what you eat for breakfast, lunch, dinner, and snacks or desserts. It may also be useful to note the time you eat, the amount of food you eat, and how many grams of carbohydrates the food contains. Healthy habits like these can help you manage your blood glucose levels, inform your doctor about your diet, and keep you honest about your everyday food choices.

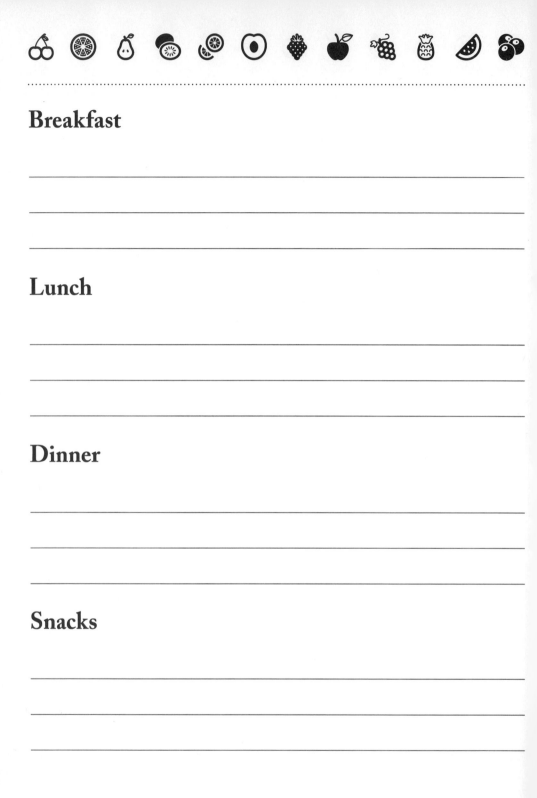

Breakfast

_____

_____

_____

Lunch

_____

_____

_____

Dinner

_____

_____

_____

Snacks

_____

_____

_____

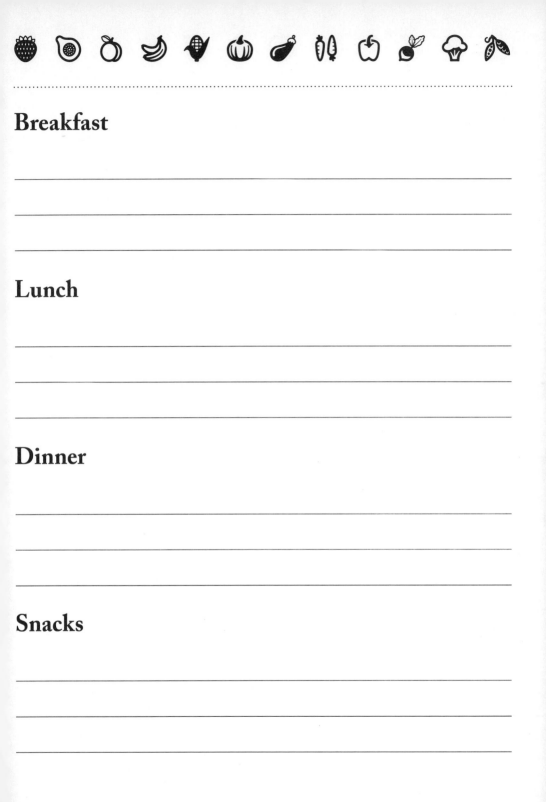

Breakfast

Lunch

Dinner

Snacks

Breakfast

_____

_____

_____

Lunch

_____

_____

_____

Dinner

_____

_____

_____

Snacks

_____

_____

_____

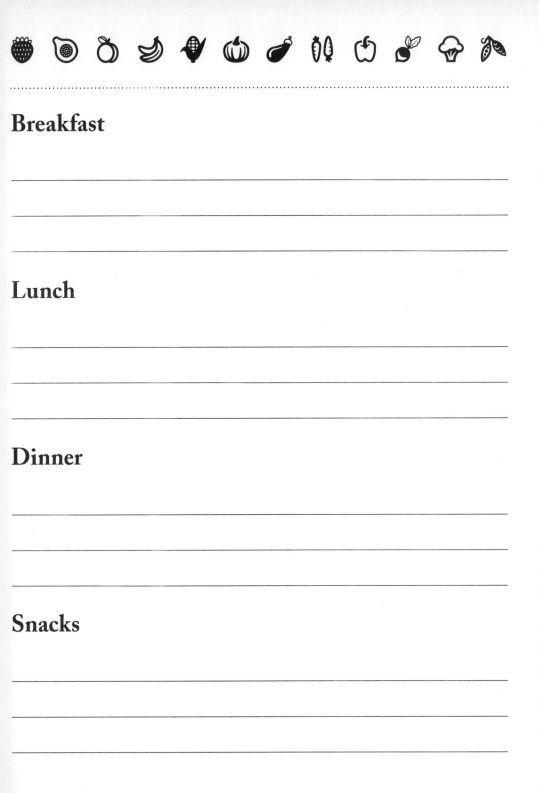

Breakfast

_____

_____

_____

Lunch

_____

_____

_____

Dinner

_____

_____

_____

Snacks

_____

_____

_____

Index